I0569084

The Musical Looking Glass

Note-Reading and Early Piano Fluency *through* Singing, Guided Discovery, & Creative Play

by Elise Winters & Hollie Thomas

KALEIDOSCOPES
FOR VIOLIN

The Musical Looking Glass: Note-Reading & Early Piano Fluency Through Singing, Guided Discovery, and Creative Play; by Elise Winters & Hollie Thomas

© 2025 Kaleidoscopes for Violin, Austin, Texas.

ISBN 978-1-959675-12-9

Table of Contents

■ Piano literacy / fluency   ■ Kaleidoscopes repertoire song   ■ Note-reading / rhythm

User Guide

The Musical Looking Glass is divided essentially into four parts which are interleaved throughout the book, and distinguished by the color of their titles throughout the book and in the Table of Contents:

Piano Fluency Pieces & Activities: This broad category includes three kinds of activities:

Explorations: Short, semi-structured pieces with an improvisatory element. These offer a tonal framework and artistic direction without being overly determined. This format allows the student to exercise their own creativity while experiencing a sense of satisfying music-making. Pedagogically the pieces fulfill three roles:

1. Increasing students' visual fluency and dexterity on the piano;
2. Providing a rewarding aesthetic experience; and
3. Offering a palette of pleasing and accessible sounds or patterns, which set students on a path toward further melodic and harmonic exploration.

Repertoire: Six child-friendly folk songs (e.g. Hot Cross Buns, Naughty Kitty Cat) offer an enjoyable way for students to build solfege fluency. These songs also form the basis for other literacy activities such as the Rhythm Puzzles.

Games: Several non-musical games offer a fun way to reinforce piano fluency and/or literacy.

Note-Reading: These exercises, beginning with "Cobblestone Streets" on page 21, are simple, predictable, melodies composed by Elise Winters. They are designed to build students' reading and sight-singing abilities in the following ways:

- *The melodies played on the piano with both hands in parallel*, building manual dexterity alongside note-reading.
- *The melodies are simultaneously sung in moveable-*do *solfege* (i.e. naming the notes by scale degree). The singing builds their sense of pitch and vocal control, while the solfege helps them to internalize the relationships among notes.
- *The use of "do clef" notation* (see _)allows the notated music to be notated in a variety of apparent keys, while still being sung in the child's preferred range.

Rhythm Activities: Two main types of rhythm activities are included:

- **Rhythm Puzzles:** Activities in which students discover and practice the interrelationship between rhythm and beat, using beat circles; and
- **Additional Activities**: Flash cards and rhythm echoes can be used to internalize the sound and notation of four fundamental rhythms: ♩ ♫ ♬ 𝄾 using the "ta ka te ka" system.

The various activities are presented in the book in an approximate order students might be expected to progress. However, the journey of any individual student will be unique, depending on their particular interests, strengths, and challenges.

Some Notes About the Activities

Most of the piano activities use a partner. If the activity is being done within a private instrumental or vocal lesson, this will be the teacher; at home it will likely be the parent; in a group setting, it will be another student. The term "partner" refers to any of these configurations. The activities are designed to provide an enjoyable musical experience for the partner as well as the student.

For activities in which you, the parent or teacher, are providing a musical accompaniment, you will be seated to the *left* of the student, using your *right* hand to play the pattern (since it is nearest the middle range of the piano).

While musical notation is offered on these simple accompaniments as a reminder, your teacher will model these patterns in the lesson and give you an opportunity to try them out.

Be sure to video each new activity in case you need a reminder during home practice!

The smaller text and musical notation throughout the book are intended for the parent and/or teacher.

- *Musical terms* may be introduced which are not necessarily intended to be introduced yet to the student. Some of these terms are explained in the Glossary on page vi.

- *Music notation* is introduced gradually throughout the book. The smaller notation in the piano activities is not necessarily a part of this — it is merely intended as a guide to the teacher and parent. The student is not expected to read or understand this.

  Students may naturally be curious about the notation they are seeing! It is great for them to *see* musical notation in their daily environment without the expectation that they read it — just as they encountered written words well before they began to read. It is fine to answer any questions they have about what any of these symbols mean.

Vocabulary. For each concept introduced in this book, the *underlying concept*, rather than its formal name, are the primary learning goal. While specialized musical terms may occasionally be used to provide clarity for the teacher and/or parent, introducing these to students is optional.

The teacher may share musical terms as desired with any older or more musically experienced student who is using the book.

Note Writing

For the purposes of this book, "writing" music refers to any method of visually indicating notes and rhythms. For students of all ages, and especially younger students, using *physical manipulatives* are faster and easier than drawing and filling in note heads. Mistakes can be corrected in a single move, rather than erasing and re-drawing.

This instructional adaptation allows the focus to remain on the concept itself rather than the physical act of writing. Similarly, "stick notation" is used in the rhythm section for ease and simplicity.

Traditional notation, including note heads and physically drawing notes on the staff, will be introduced in the next volume.

Integrating into Lessons

The note-reading activities can be done in a few minutes of lesson time, and are easy enough that the student can work through them independently with occasional check-ins.

The piano activities are an enjoyable and valuable lesson activity. They may take a bit longer (10–15 minutes), but will provide hours of enjoyment for student and parent at home.

They are also suited perfectly to group class, with up to three students on a single piano.

Tracking Assignments

Blue boxes are provided in the top corner of each page to track when various activities are begun and completed. The number of boxes corresponds to the number of steps in the assignment.

Your teacher may choose to leave out a given activity, perhaps returning to it at a later time. These choices are flexible, and depend on their teaching priorities as well as the interest and developmental readiness of the student.

A Few Musical Terms

Below are explanations of some of the terms used throughout the book. These are not intended to be comprehensive dictionary definitions — rather, they offer functional and approachable ways to understand the terms.

Scale, Melody, and Note Relationship Terms

Melody consists of notes arranged sequentially to create an aural sense of line. The line can rise or fall, and can even have some steep hills and valleys — as long as our ear perceives them to be part of a shared contour.

Key refers to the set of notes chosen for a piece, including which note is serving as "home." Although the piano has 12 distinct notes, each *key* typically only uses seven of these. *Diatonic notes* are the notes which are used in a particular chosen key.

Do take note that the individual notes on a piano are also called *keys*. So we can, for example, say that C Major is a special *key* because it uses only the white *keys* of a piano.

A *scale* is the full set of notes in a particular key, in stepwise order. A note's position within a given scale, expressed as a number, is called the *scale degree*. So for example, in an A scale, the second scale degree is B.

Solfege is the language used to describe melodic relationships. It is another way of naming the degrees of the scale.

Transposition is moving a melody onto another "home note" — for example, starting "Twinkle, Twinkle" on D instead of A. When a melody is transposed, the alphabetic notes change, but the solfege (as well as the relative relationships among the notes) stays the same.

Interval is the diatonic distance between two notes, expressed as a number. From one note to the next note is defined as a *second*. Below are a few particularly important intervals:

- *Half step:* The closest distance between two notes. This might be from a white key to a neighboring black key, or between two white keys.
- *Whole step*: The next-closest distance between two notes. On piano, this looks like two notes which have one key in between them.
- *Thirds*: The distance from one note of the scale to *two* notes away — i.e. a "skip." This harmonious sound is the basis for all chords.

- *Fifths*: Notes which are five notes apart, including the top and bottom note. The outside two notes of a *triad* are a fifth.
- *Octave*: Notes which have matching sounds, like low C and high C. The higher note is *eight* diatonic notes from the lower note — hence the name *octave*. When played together, the two notes seem to blend into one.

Chord and Harmony Terms

Chord: a set of three or more notes arranged in *skips*, or *thirds*. Chords are used to create a background, or *harmony*, for the melody.

The notes of a chord may be played simultaneously or sequentially. It is also fine to leave out certain notes and to move notes into different octaves. Regardless of the configuration, it is still the same chord.

A chord can even be the *imagined* background of a melody. When we hear a melody, our minds automatically fill in this context. The implied chord *could* be played, even if it isn't physically there right now — like the implied "I will" in the phrase, "See you later."

So we can say, "'This melody starts on the tonic chord" — even if it a solo melody and no one has ever played chords with it. *Our mind naturally supplies a chordal context* because the melody itself contains the clues.

An *arpeggio* is an example of one way of playing a chord, turning it into a curving row of notes that sounds like a melody! Many piano pieces don't have a melody per se, but are made primarily out of arpeggios.

Tonic: The "home" note of a key. A melody will almost always end on tonic; and the last chord of a piece will almost always be the tonic chord.

Arpeggio: The notes of a chord, played *sequentially* (rather than simultaneously) and *in order* (although some notes may be skipped).

Triad: The notes of a chord, arranged in order from lowest to highest.

Some Notes About Piano & Piano Technique

Piano is used in this book as a literacy instrument. While developing technique and form is not the primary focus, having some essentials of good form, as well as an adequate instrument, will provide the student with a more musically rewarding experience and a better foundation for future development.

Choosing a Piano

To make the most of this book, students will need a piano in their home. Essential features include *weighted keys* and *velocity sensitivity* (i.e. the keys respond to the touch of the player.) An 88-key (7-octave) range provides a greater palette of color and sound, and allows plenty of room for the partner and student to play side-by-side.

A *sustain pedal, (damper pedal)*, is essential to create a legato sound, as well as to create ambience. If using a plug-in pedal, a weighted version can be purchased separately and provides greater comfort and stability.

Many piano teachers find that the Roland FPX-30X or equivalent meets a minimum standard for students' first several years of exploration and study. This is a desktop model with a satisfying touch and a beautiful sound. For a modestly larger investment, a quality floor-standing piano will represent a significant upgrade, and offer years of musical enjoyment.

Learning Melodies in D Major

While many parents may have begun their own piano studies in C major, students will play their first melodies (songs such as Hot Cross Buns and Let Us Chase the Squirrel) in D major for the following reasons:

1. A child who does not yet know left and right can find *do* much more easily in D major, since *do* is located *between* the two black keys.
2. The hand position is more natural, the tallest finger being on a black key; and
3. It is the easiest key for children to sing.

Introducing DO clef

Students first note-reading exercises (see "Cobblestone Streets" on page 21) are notated using DO clef (see figure 1). This allows the music to be written in various locations on the staff without the use of sharps or flats. *In this book, "do" will always be D. They will simultaneously sing the note names in mov-*

able-do solfege. Staying in D major builds students' audiation ability within their natural vocal range.

Placing the Hands in D Major

Do clef is used to mark the location of *do*.

For the D Major songs and exercises, the THUMB of the right hand is placed on the note D. Each finger is placed on a white key, except the middle finger which is placed on F♯.

For the left hand, the PINKY is placed on D. The middle finger will still be F♯.

In piano playing, by contrast to most string and wind instruments, the thumb as well as the fingers are numbered. Students readily understand and adjust to this difference.

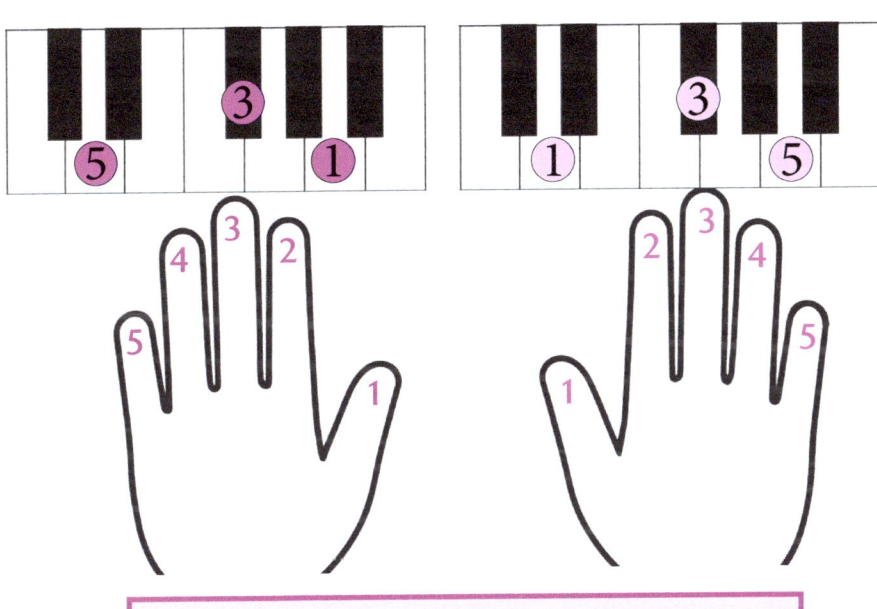

For activities using both the left and right hand, the DARKER circles are used to indicate the left hand, which is often playing lower notes.

Establishing a Correct Seated Position

A good seated position is essential for comfort, fluency, and avoiding strain in the wrists and forearms.

- *The feet must be able to rest on the floor*. Add a footstool if necessary to achieve the correct height. This is essential for a tall, straight back, which allows the arms to move freely. *Have you ever sat on a tall barstool which was missing the foot rung? This is what a child is experiencing when their feet can't touch the floor!*

- *The bench must be the correct height*. Raise the bench high enough that the arms form a right angle when resting the hands on the keys. Use a firm pad or books if necessary.

- *The back should be tall yet relaxed*. This allows for the free movement of the arms. Use the language "tall back" to encourage a lengthening of the spine, rather than "straight back," which tends to lead to over-arching.

A Few Technique Essentials

As students begin playing melodies, their starting hand position will consist of *one finger resting on each scale note*. In this position, observe the following points:

- The wrists should be gently lifted.
- The overall hand shape should be soft and rounded.
- The fingers may contact the piano key in a variety of places — on the fingertip, pad, or somewhere in between. This will depend on the length of the finger and the note being played.
- Contrary to what one might assume, the playing motion is not *typing* with individual fingers but rather *dropping* or *rolling* into each finger with the resting weight of the arm.

  Put another way, the arm weight is directed *into* the finger, rather than the fingers moving individually.

  For this reason, the wrist should remain loose, pivoting subtly from side to side, aligned with the finger being played. *While this motion is not a focus of the book, simply having a loose wrist will facilitate this natural function.*

- To move the hand from location to location, the *wrist* will lift the hand and fingers; these are allowed to hang loosely.

Use books to raise the seat to the correct height, and place a stool under your child's feet for support.

A Word About Independent Fingering

When first introduced to the piano, a young child will naturally use just their index finger to play each note. This finger is much easier for them to isolate and aim. They are welcome to continue doing this until they have the attention and coordination to move to independent fingering. The younger the child, the longer this will take.

Many of the activities in this book are designed to build independent fingering ability bit by bit. These activities include suggested fingerings.

For activities with no fingering specified, any fingering may be used.

The Kaleidoscopes Repertoire

Six songs from the Kaleidoscopes repertoire album are used to develop piano fluency and solfege singing. These are folk songs and will already be familiar to many children.

Parents are suggested to play the Kaleidoscopes reference recording daily for a month or two in order to acquaint the child with these songs. The child can also enjoy singing the song and following along with the pictorial notation. The album includes the movable-*do* solfege (a way of naming the scale degrees) which will be used to learn the songs on the piano.

When students begin playing them on piano, do this primarily by ear. In other words, keep the book closed! If a refresher is needed, sing them a few times, and provide the solfege verbally, phrase by phrase, as needed.

The Kaleidoscopes album is available to stream on Spotify, Apple Music, and other major platforms. The album is also available on compact disc.

FOLLOW THE LINKS TO LISTEN TO KALEIDOSCOPES BOOK 1

APPLE MUSIC

SPOTIFY

YOUTUBE MUSIC

Concepts Included in Volume 1

Below are some important concepts introduced in this book. Of these, some are formally named; others are named using accessible language — for example, note values are named using rhythm language rather than their fractional names — and still others are experienced but not yet made conscious or named.

It is the choice of the teacher when to introduce the musical vocabulary used throughout the book, always adding the vocabulary only *after* the underlying concept has been explored and revealed.

Rhythmic Concepts

Steady beat

Distinguishing rhythm and beat

♩ and ♫

Four-beat measures in duple meter

Melodic Concepts

Higher and lower

Steps and skips

Naming and audiating the lower tetrachord: DO-SO

The major scale

Phrase endings on the tonic

Four-bar phrase structure

Coordinating a note or melody with a 2-, 3-, or 4-beat accompanimental pattern

Half steps and whole steps (as a sound)

Note and Notation Concepts

The musical staff

Organization of notes on the staff

Alphabetic note names on the piano

Octave equivalence

Half steps and whole steps (as a distance)

Sharp note names

Fluency with the order of the alphabetic note names in ascending and descending directions

Harmonic Concepts

The experience of an accompanimental pattern coupled with a treble melody

Tritone (as a sound)

Chords & Arpeggios

The diatonic chords of the major scale (as an experience)

Open fifths, as a harmonic color

Tonic, as an experience of returning to a place of harmonic rest

Simple 2-, 3- and 4-note chord progressions or loops

Physical Skills

Visually navigating the musical staff

Visually navigating the piano keyboard

Independent fingering

Coordinating both hands in parallel

Crossover fingering

Playing thirds with alternating fingers

Playing fifths with outside fingers

Playing a root-position triad

You must have a room, or a certain hour or so a day,
where you don't know what was in the newspapers that morning,
you don't know who your friends are, you don't know what you owe anybody,
you don't know what anybody owes to you.

This is a place where you can simply experience and bring forth
what you are and what you might be.
This is the place of creative incubation.

At first you may find that nothing happens there.
But if you have a sacred place and use it, something eventually will happen.

– Joseph Campbell, *The Power of Myth*

The Adventure Begins...

MUSICAL JELLYFISH

Objective: Using the wrist to transport the hand around the piano

FLOATING JELLYFISH

Musical accompaniment: "Aquarium" from Carnival of the Animals by Camille Saint-Saëns.

Practice moving both hands like jellyfish, using a large motion, while standing or walking around the room.

FLYING JELLYFISH

PART 1

Use the THIRD (middle) finger of either hand to play any black key. Your practice partner will provide a musical accompaniment. The speed and timing are not important — just have fun flying and landing.

How adventurous is your jellyfish? How far can it travel from one note to the next? Make sure to lift from the wrist each time.

Try the same thing with the other hand!

PART 2

When you're ready, try landing on *two adjacent notes* — a black key, and either of the neighboring white keys! Use the SECOND and THIRD fingers.

It is easiest to play the notes simultaenously. Later, try playing them consecutively! Which sound do you like?

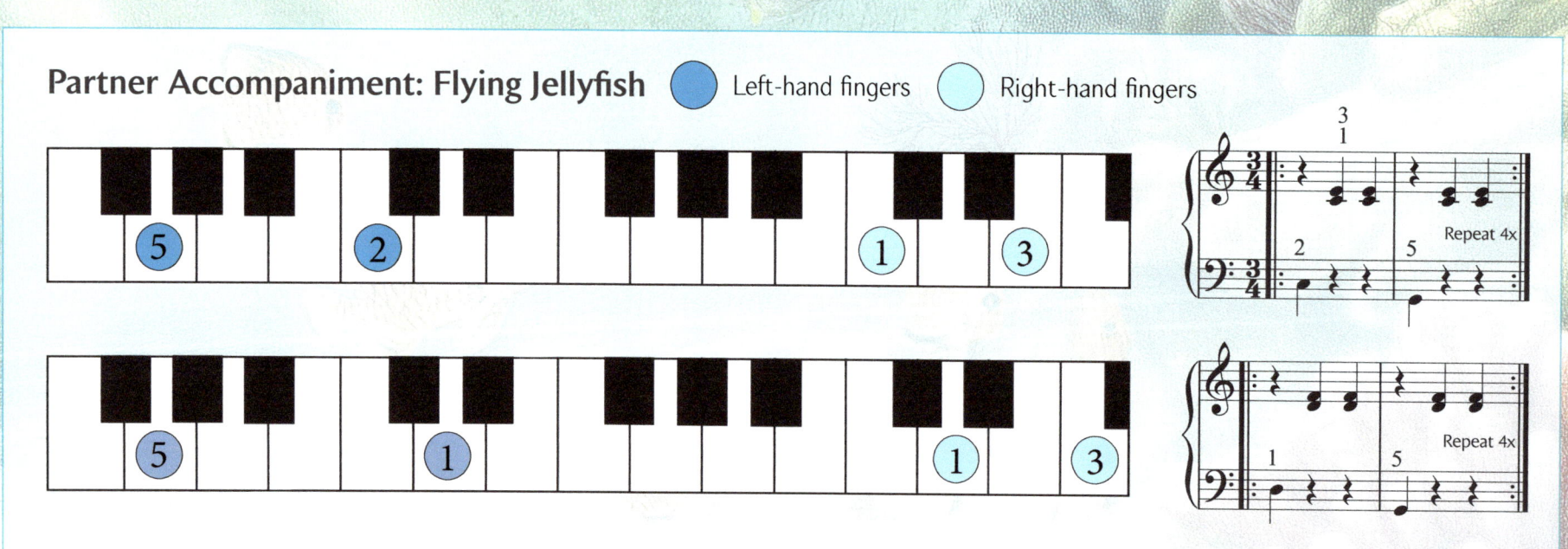

Partner Accompaniment: Flying Jellyfish ● Left-hand fingers ○ Right-hand fingers

GIRAFFES & ELEPHANTS

Objective: Distinguishing groupings of two and three; using independent fingers.

PREPARATION: Place a flat eraser on each set of adjacent white keys, near the top of the keys. Do this on ALL octaves of the piano.

1. Play all the BLACK keys in order from left to right, using the RIGHT hand. It is okay to use just one finger in the beginning.

   For each group of three, say, "elephant" (three syllables). For each group of two, say "giraffe" (two syllables).

2. Do the same thing using the LEFT hand!

GIRAFFE JAMBOREE

Now practice finding ONLY giraffes. Do it first with the RIGHT hand, then the left. It is okay to use the pointer finger in the beginning. When you are ready:

1. Use the SECOND and THIRD fingers.
2. Use a wrist motion to move the hand from group to group.

ELEPHANT ENTOURAGE

Once you've done that, now practice finding ONLY elephants. Do it first with the RIGHT hand, then the left. Again, it's okay to use just the pointer finger in the beginning. Try these additional upgrades when you are ready:

1. Use the *three middle fingers* (i.e. excluding the thumb and pinky).
2. Use a wrist motion to move from group to group.

 Left-hand fingers   Right-hand fingers

DIVIDED HANDS

Combine both hands, using the left hand in the low register and the right hand in the high register. Do "Giraffe Jamboree" first, then "Elephant Entourage."

CORAL, FISH & SHARK

Before you begin, MARK the adjacent white keys (natural half-steps) with erasers, to help the black key groupings stand out more easily.

THE CORAL

The "coral" notes will use the THUMB and THIRD finger. Play these notes in various places in the UPPER half of the piano.

Try playing these notes 1) separately (this is easier), then 2) simultaneously (which is a bit harder).

The practice partner can use the sustain pedal to create a peaceful, shimmery feeling.

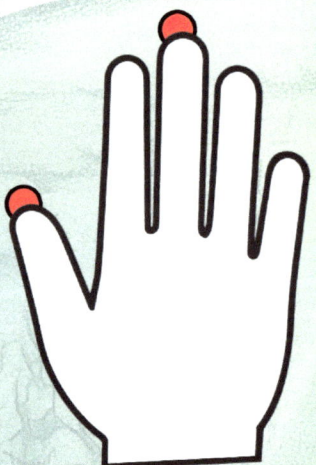

THE SHARK

Objective: Reliably and quickly locating specific notes on the piano keyboard.

There is a shark roaming the ocean!

Play the notes on the outside of each group of three black keys ("elephant"). Use the THUMB and FOURTH finger of each hand. Play the two notes simultaneously.

Find the shark in many places in the piano.

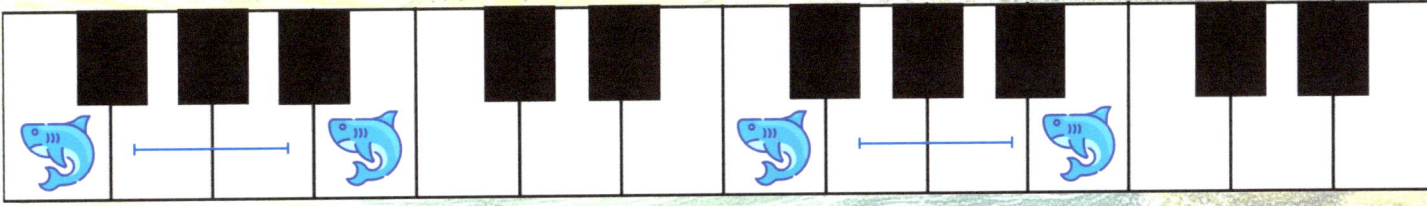

THE DELTA FISH

Let's meet some fish! The easiest to find is D, which is in the center of a "giraffe." We'll call this a *delta fish*.

Find all the same kinds of fish on the keyboard. Use your THIRD finger to play each one.

The practice partner should should hold the sustain pedal to blend the sounds of these matching notes.

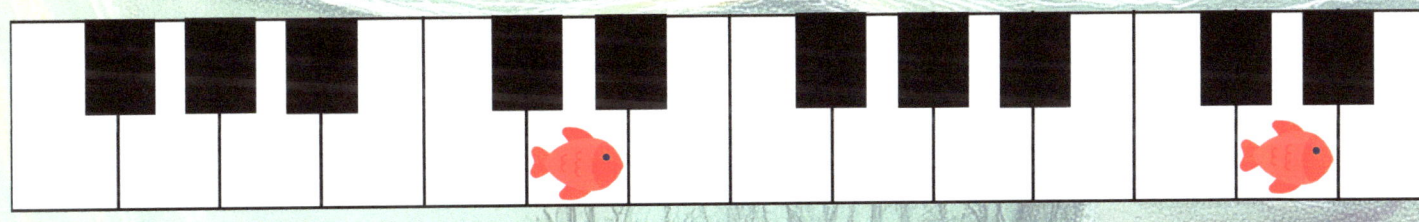

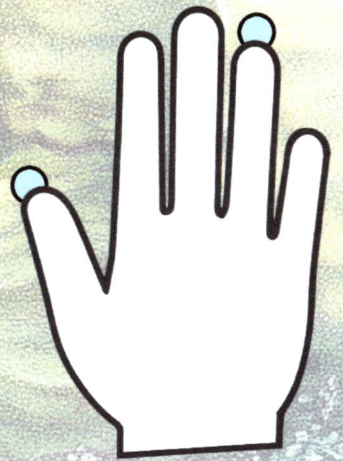

FIND THE HIDDEN FISH

Now try finding these notes, in order. Use an eraser to mark ONE location of the desired note on the keyboard, as a visual template.

C (clownfish)   E (emperor)

F (firefish)   G (goatfish)

B (betta)   A (angelfish)

5

Hot Cross Buns

M R D ~ M R D ~

M R D ~

r r r r

d d d

Let Us Chase the Squirrel

S

M

m m

r r

r r

r r

d d

d d

d d

S

M

r r

r r

d d

d d

D ~

Play the songs on these pages and page 17 on piano in the key of D Major, using the Kaleidoscopes recording to learn them by ear.

Boil Them Cabbage Down

Mary Had a Little Lamb

A RAINY EVENING

Use any keys on the piano to create the sound of a rainstorm.

Explore various sounds — high & low, short & long, loud & soft.

What might the following sound like?

RAINDROPS   RAIN   THUNDER   LIGHTNING   WIND

Continue developing your piece a little bit each day. Use the area below to write down each section of your piece if you wish.

Once you are done, create a recording to share with a family member.

The rain came down, straight and silvery, like a punishment of steel rods. It clattered onto the house and onto the rocks and pitted the sea. The thunder made some sounds like grand pianos falling downstairs, then settled to a softer continuous rumble, which was almost drowned by the sound of the rain. The flashes of lightning joined into long illuminations which made the grass a lurid green, the rocks a blazing ochre yellow.

– from The Sea, The Sea, *by Iris Murdoch*

Hot Cross Buns Rhythm
Puzzle (in lesson)

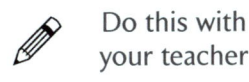

Do this with your teacher

The instructions for this activity can be found on page 13.

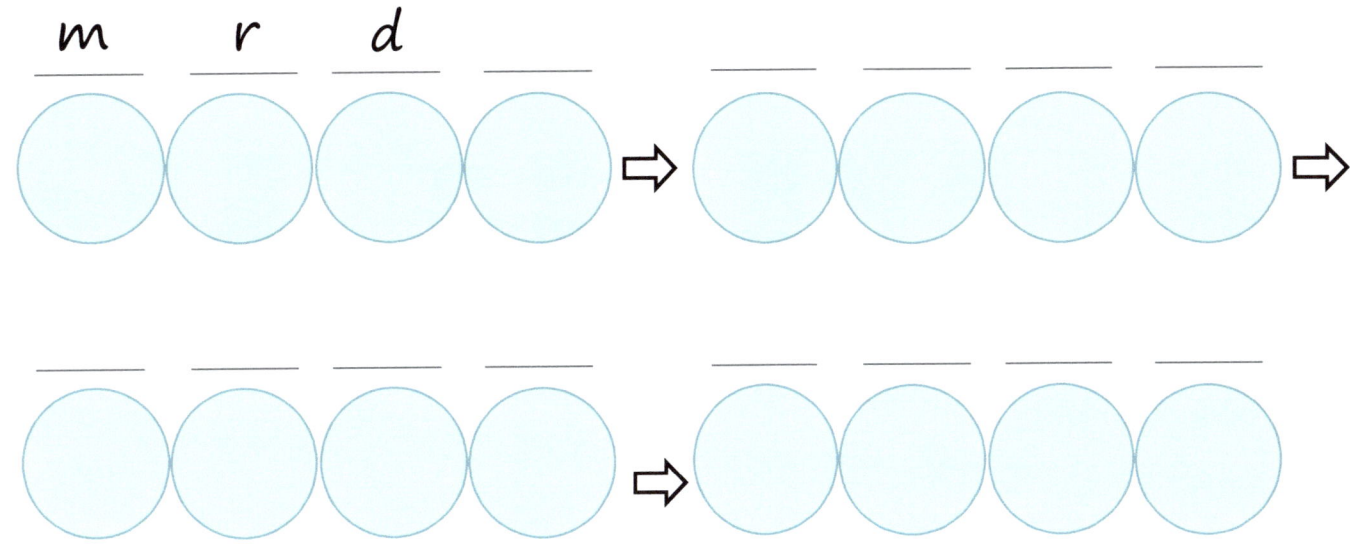

m   r   d

THE WESTMINSTER CHIMES

Objective: Practicing independent fingers

The Westminster Chimes, or Cambridge Chimes, are located at the Church of St. Mary the Great, at the Palace of Westminster in Cambridge, England. The clock tower marks each quarter of an hour by playing a melody on the four "quarter bells" inside. A different melody is used for each quarter hour. This allows people to know the time even if they are not within sight of the clock.

On celebration days and for special events, the chimes are rung randomly by the bell-ringer. Enjoy creating this joyful hubbub!

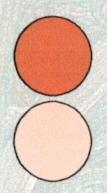

Left-hand fingers

Right-hand fingers

Partner Note: In piano writing, the stem direction may be used to indicate which hand plays each of the notes. UPWARD stems indicate the right hand; DOWNWARD stems indicate the left.

THE CHIME MELODY

This is the melody which is played at the top of each hour.

STRIKING THE HOURS (BIG BEN)

Use all four notes to mark the hour — one strike for each hour.

The notes here are just an example. Don't try to read them — just make a lot of noise!

CELEBRATION

Play all the notes in any order and combination.

10

Three-Note Patterns • Name the Lines & Spaces

Objective: Placing the notes DO, RE and MI; identifying lines and spaces by number.

Use coins, erasers, or beads to practice the following concepts:

1. The alternation of line notes and space notes,
2. Placing *do*, *re*, and *mi* in various patterns,
3. Identifying notes on lines, by number,
4. Identifying notes on spaces, by number; and
5. Identifying notes on both lines and spaces.

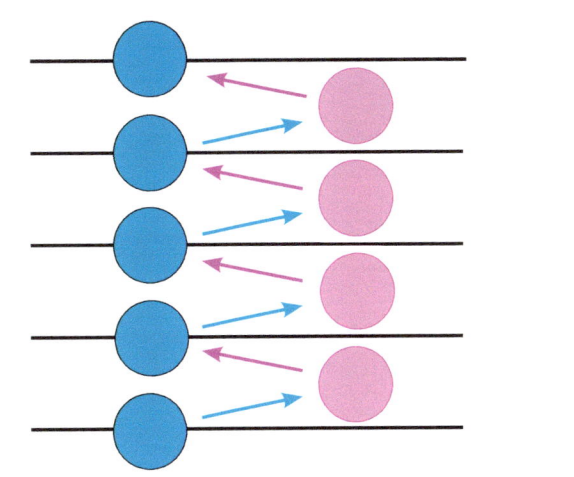

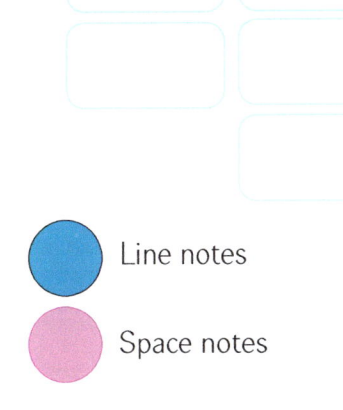

Line notes

Space notes

11

MISTY MORNING

PREPARATION: Mark the natural half-steps as before, in all the octaves of the piano.

MIST ON THE POND

Now use erasers to mark the white keys surrounding a "giraffe," on the LOWEST octave of the piano. This will serve as a visual template.

Play these notes in many places on the piano in an ascending pattern. Use BOTH hands — whichever is closer to the notes you are playing — using fingers 1, 2 and 3.

The practice partner can the sustain pedal to create the "misty" sound.

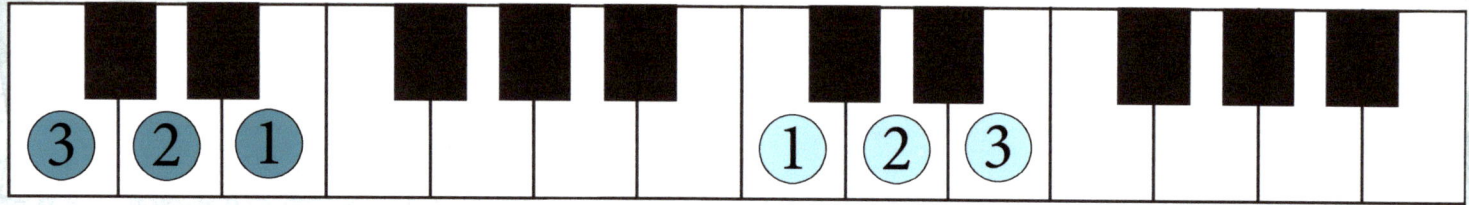

BIRDS FLYING OVERHEAD

Mark the G just below middle C, as a template. You will be using all of the G's HIGHER than this one on the piano.

Play each G twice with the FOURTH finger. (Let's practice finding this finger!) Do this in many octaves, using the upper half of the piano. Do you hear the birds overhead?

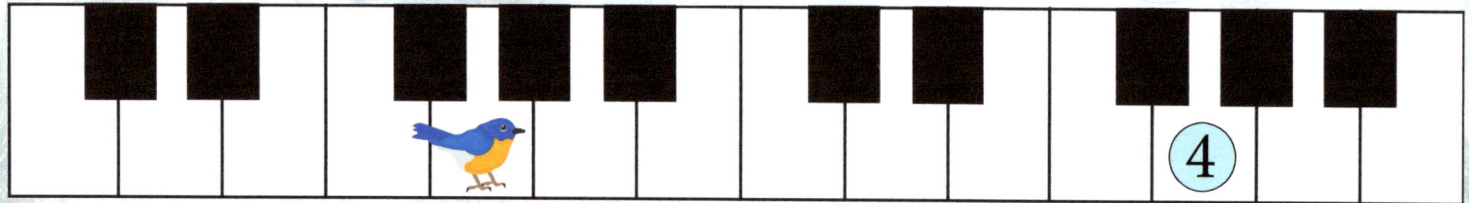

What else would you like to add to your scene or story? What will it sound like?

12

RHYTHM PUZZLE: Hot Cross Buns

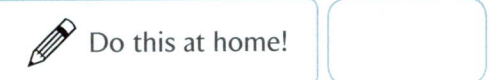 Do this at home!

1. Sing the song using the solfège words to the song. Keep the beat using a lap-tap movement.

2. Sing the song again. This time, tap your pencil on the circles below, moving from left to right.

3. Are there any beats that have NO sounds? *Draw a squiggle or Z in these circles.*

4. Sing the song again, tapping across the beats. Are there any beats that have only ONE sound? *Write a single line in these circles.*

5. Sing the song again. What do you hear on the remaining circles? *Fill these in.*

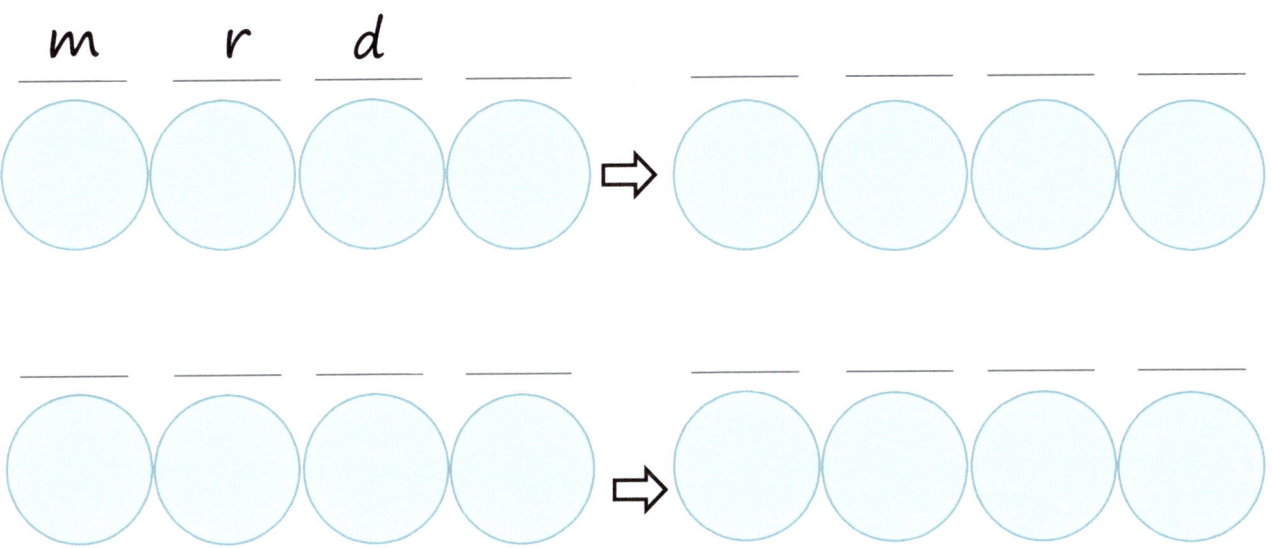

The blanks above the notes can be used to write the solfege note names, if desired.

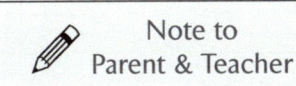 Note to Parent & Teacher

Learning Through Guided Discovery

It is tempting to help your child get the right answer on these exercises. However, it is much *more* important that they figure this out *on their own*.

Rather than pointing out their mistakes, you can instead guide them to *discovering* the mismatch.

A great way to help them do this is to sing the words of the song *in the rhythm they wrote*. This might mean leaving out words, singing two notes faster, etc.

Since the song is already familiar to them, they will find it highly entertaining to hear this funny, "wrong" version of the song. They'll be determined to figure out how to make the song come out correct.

The method above should be used predominantly.

There is also another method which can be used occasionally once the child is quite experienced with rhythm puzzles. The parent or teacher can say, "There is a mistake in the [first, second, etc.] phrase. Can you find it?" Then have them sing the song again, tapping on the beat circles.

It can be useful to encourage them to "listen with their eyes."

WILBUR IN THE BARN, PART I

Text adapted from Charlotte's Web, by E.B. White

Objective: Using the 2nd and 4th fingers simultaneously; striking the keys with velocity

EARLY MORNING

The barn was still dark. The sheep lay motionless. Even the goose was quiet. Nothing stirred: the cows were resting, the horses dozed. Wilbur loved the barn when it was like this — calm and quiet, waiting for light.

Play "Mist on the Pond" from page 12.

WILBUR IS LONELY

"I have no real friend here in the barn, it's going to rain all morning and all afternoon, and Fern won't come in such bad weather. Oh, honestly!" And Wilbur the pig was crying again, for the second time in two days.

Play the marked notes in alternating pairs. Hold each pair for a long time.

Keep the tempo very slow, without using the pedal.

Carry this pattern into various octaves of the piano.

Wilbur is Lonely

THE GOOSE

"Sorry, sonny, sorry," said the goose. "I'm sitting-sitting on my eggs. Eight of them. Got to keep the toasty-oasty-oasty warm. I have to stay right here, I'm no flibberty-iberrty-gibbet. I do not play when there are eggs to hatch. I'm expecting goslings."

"Well, I didn't think you were expecting woodpeckers," said Wilbur, bitterly."

Play each pair of notes simultaneously, one hand at a time.

The goose often repeats words three times, so you will do the same thing.

Play these notes all around the piano, using both hands.

The Goose

Rhythm Puzzle: Let Us Chase the Squirrel

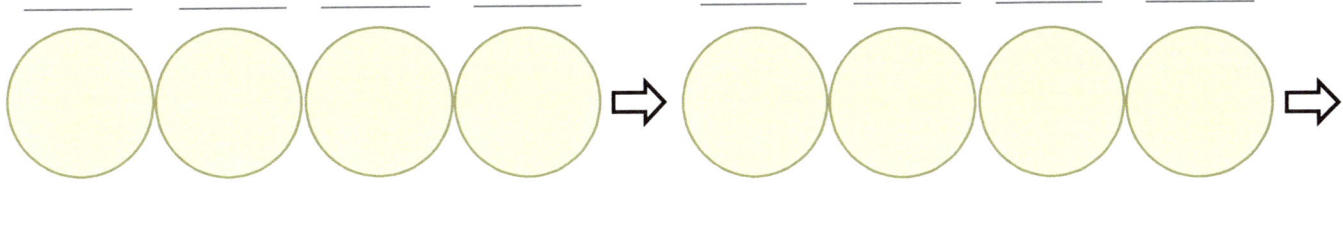

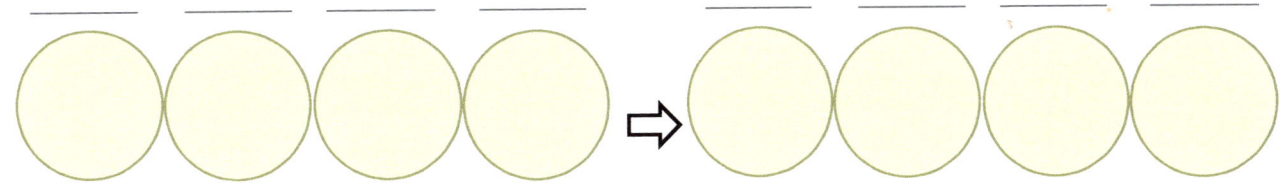

Rhythm Puzzle: Boil Them Cabbage

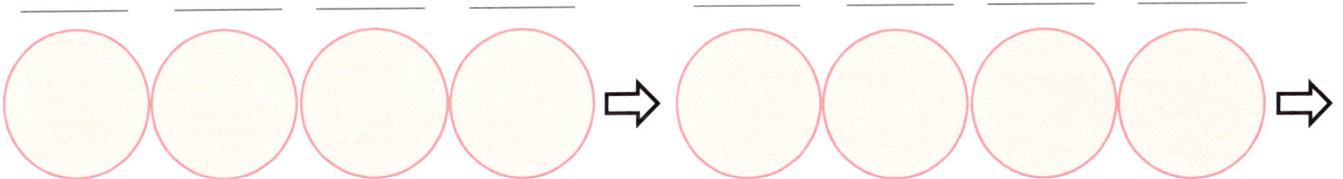

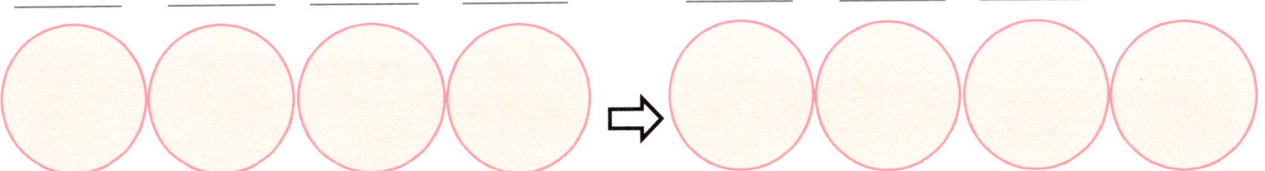

WILBUR IN THE BARN, PART II

THE GANDER

"You don't have to stay in that dirty-little dirty-little dirty-little yard," said the goose. "Go down to the garden, dig up the radishes! Root up everything! The world is a wonderful place when you're young."

Find pairs of white keys and black keys. Play each pair three times, simultaneously.

Use the LEFT hand, in the LOWEST octave of the piano.

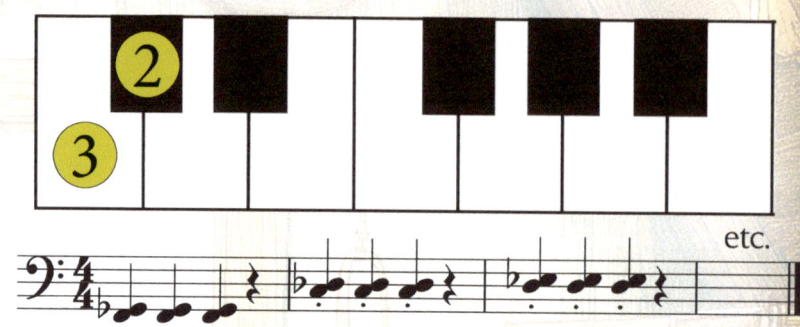

TEMPLETON IN THE TUNNELS

Templeton, the rat, crept stealthily along the wall and disappeared into a private tunnel. He had tunnels and runways all over the farm and could get from one place to another without being seen.

1. Mark the two E's just below the middle of the piano.

2. Now play ALL the keys in between — black and white, using the SECOND and THIRD fingers of both hands. Each hand will play just TWO notes.

Play this in a variety of octaves.

A QUIET VOICE FROM THE CORNER

Just as Wilbur was settling down for his morning nap, he heard again the voice that had addressed him the night before. "Salutations!" said the voice.

At last Wilbur saw the creature that had spoken to him in such a kindly way. Stretched across the upper part of the doorway was a big spiderweb, and hanging from the top of the web, head down, was a large grey spider. She had eight legs, and she was waving one of them at Wilbur.

"See me now?" she asked. "My name is Charlotte."

What does Charlotte's music sound like? You decide!

Mark your notes on the keyboard, using a small circle for each note.

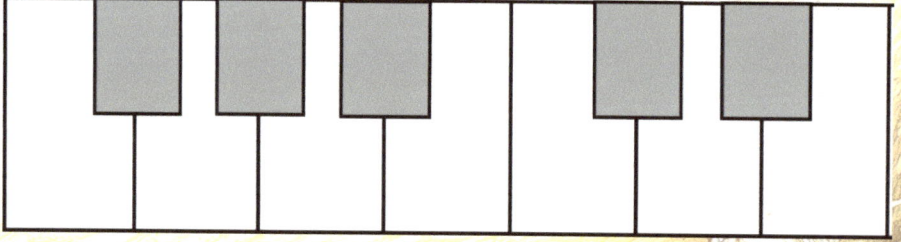

16

All Around the Buttercup

Naughty Kitty Cat

THE SECRET GARDEN, PART I

Objective: Exploring the piano melodically within a simple, harmonically flexible chord progression.

Text adapted from The Secret Garden, by Frances Hodgson Burnett

Mary slipped through the door and shut it behind her, and stood with her back against it, looking about her with wonder and delight. She was standing INSIDE the secret garden.

The high walls which shut it in were covered with climbing roses, still bare from winter. In the ten years that the garden had been untended, the roses had grown across the trees, making bridges from branch to branch and hanging in curtains of brown and gray vine.

"How still it is!" she whispered. "How still!"

The robin, who had flown to his treetop, was still as all the rest. He did not even flutter his wings; he sat without stirring, and looked at Mary.

"No wonder it is still," she whispered again. "I am the first person who has spoken in here for ten years."

THE WINTER GARDEN

Improvise on WHITE keys in the upper half of the piano while your partner plays the accompaniment pattern at the right. Work toward staying aligned with the beat.

Which note makes a satisfying ending?

When you are ready for a change, the partner can play a different accompaniment pattern. This can dramatically change the mood! The teacher can provide some options for varying the accompaniment.

THE SONG OF THE ROBIN

What sound does the robin make as the robin hops from branch to branch? Does the accompaniment change or stay the same during the robin's music?

Partner Accompaniment: The Winter Garden

The practice partner will alternate between D minor and A minor chords, played just below middle C, in a broken pattern. Each pattern is played THREE times.

Repeat this sequence many times while the student improvises a melody.

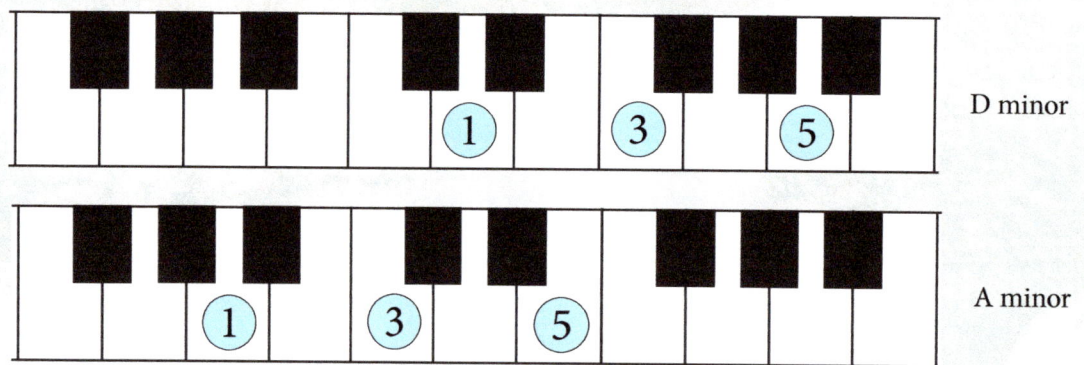

Play the chord in a broken pattern:

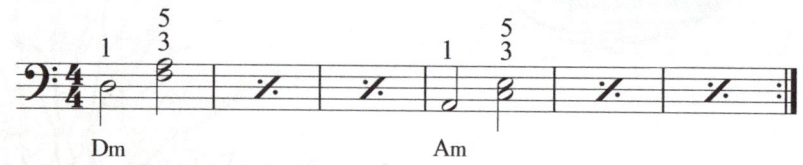

The ⁒ sign is an indication to repeat the previous measure.

18

RHYTHM PUZZLE: Mary Had a Little Lamb

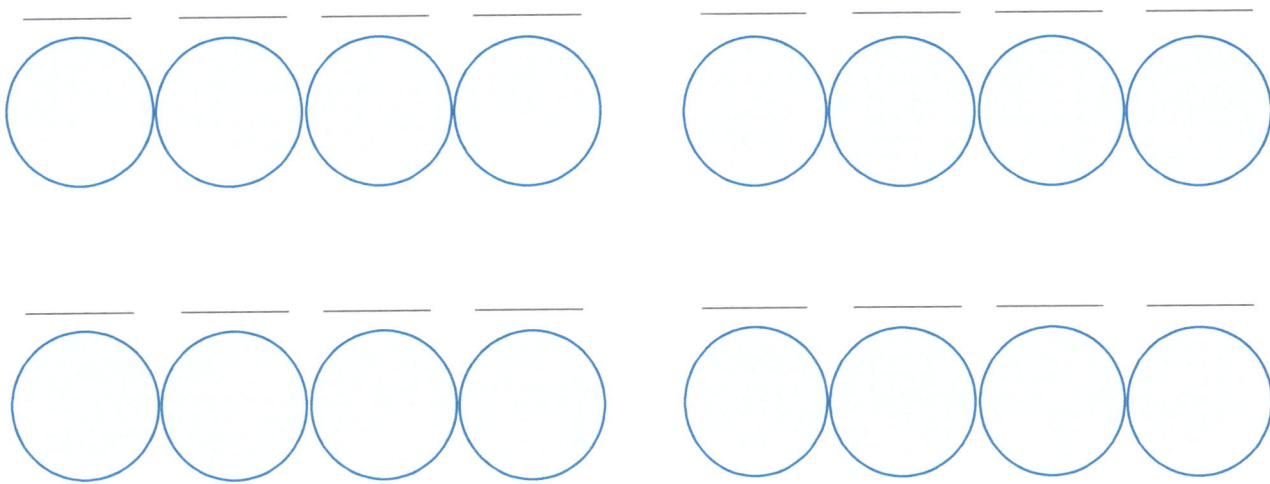

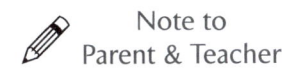
Note to Parent & Teacher

Don't Give Away the Answer!

Your teacher may begin doing Rhythm Echoes and Rhythm Flash Card with your child at this point in the book. This awareness and vocabulary from these activities will complement the Rhythm Puzzle activity!

However, make sure to preserve the purity of the Rhythm Puzzles as a musical discovery experience.

In other words, while you may want to be helpful and say, "Listen to this beat — can you hear that it's a *ta te*?", it is necessary to give the child room to have this realization on their own, following the steps outlined on "Rhythm Puzzle: Hot Cross Buns" on page 13.

The goal is for the child to discover the pattern *for themselves*, rather than recognizing them from hindsight, after the adult has already revealed the answer.

19

THE SECRET GARDEN, PART II

Objective: Using the 1st and 5th finger together in the interval of a fifth; interacting melodically with a waltz pattern

A MYSTERIOUS SOUND

Mary tucked her feet under her and made herself comfortable. "Listen to the' wind wutherin' round the house," Martha said.

Mary did not know what "wutherin'" meant until she listened. It must mean that hollow shuddering sort of roar which rushed round and round the house as if a giant no one could see were beating at the walls and windows to try to break in.

Place the THUMB and PINKY of each hand on white keys, with THREE empty white keys between them (each with its own finger resting on it), anywhere on the keyboard. This spacing is called a *fifth*. Play the notes consecutively, in a rising pattern.

Find many places to play fifths around the piano. Listen to the hollow, empty sound of the wind.

THE GARDEN AWAKENS

Mary found the sprouting pale green points everywhere. The soil was bursting with new shoots.

And the roses — the roses! Rising out of the grass, wreathing the tree trunks and hanging from branches—they came alive day by day, hour by hour.

And flower buds—tiny at first but working Magic until they burst and uncurled into cups of scent delicately spilling themselves over their brims and filling the garden air.

As your partner plays the accompaniment, improvise a melody on WHITE keys in the upper half of the piano.

Return to this activity each day and try new ideas. Enjoy discovering sounds and melodies!

Partner Accompaniment: The Garden Awakens

The partner will alternate G and F Major chords, played just above middle C with the right hand.

The ✗ sign is an indication to repeat the previous measure.

20

Cobblestone Streets

Warm up by speaking the rhythm using TA and TA-TE while keeping a steady beat.

1. PLAY the notes below on the piano in the key of D Major, using your RIGHT hand. SING the solfege as you play. Play each line twice, or as many times as you need for it to be easy and fluent.

2. Play the melody with your LEFT hand.

3. Finally, play them both together ("copy-hands"), again singing the solfege as you play.

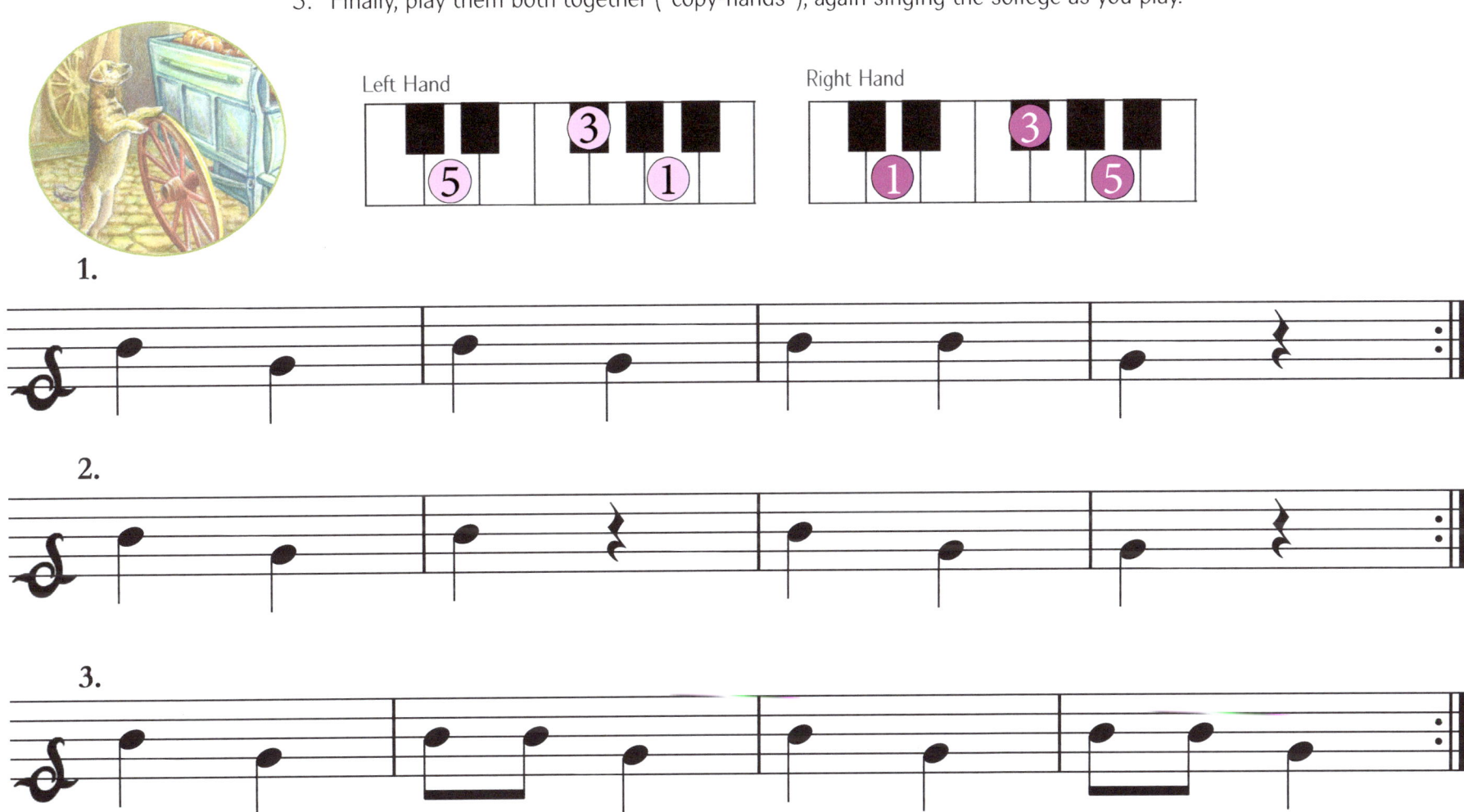

As you sing, the sound of the piano will help you find out if you sang the notes correctly. Make sure you're using your "light voice" (singing voice) rather than your "heavy voice" (speaking voice).

THE MUSICAL ALPHABET SONG

Objective: To gain fluency with the musical alphabet — ascending and descending, and starting on various letters.

A B C D E F G

1. **Solfege vs. Alphabet Names.** The names "do, re, mi," etc. go with the music and can move around. The names "A, B, C," etc. go with the piano keys and always stay the same. There are only seven notes!

2. To practice moving among these letter names in order, we sing the musical alphabet song! It uses the melody of Twinkle, but instead of all 26 letters of the actual alphabet, it uses just A–G.

3. After the first phrase of the song (you'll be singing the letter "G"), start back over at "A" to sing the second phrase. Repeat this sequence until you reach the end of the song.

4. **Change the starting letter.** Once you have done this a couple times, sing the song again, but this time starting on B. It is quite a bit harder! Use the large-print letters above to help you in the beginning.

Practice singing the song starting on EACH of the seven notes.

With each version, try getting faster and faster over the course of the song. This will test your fluency!

5. **Go backwards!** Go down the note names: "G F E D C B A." This is EVEN harder — but important to be able to do as a musician.

6. **Practice!** Over the coming week, anytime you have a few idle minutes, practice all of these versions until they are quick, fluent, and easy.

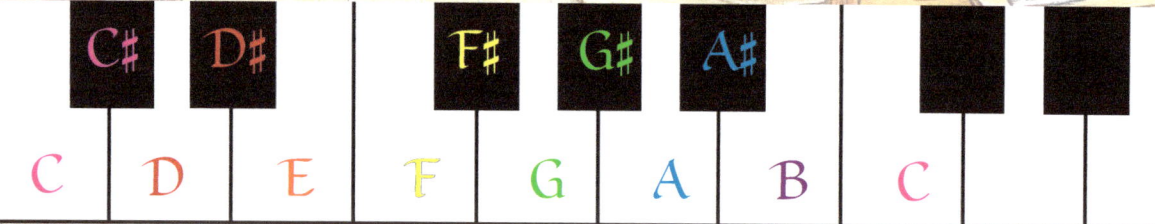

NAMING THE BLACK KEYS

Each black key is named after the white key to its left, and is one half-step higher than this note. So, for example, the note to the right of F is called "F sharp." The sharp is marked with the musical symbol ♯.

Practice saying and playing the notes in order including the black keys, starting with C.

22

Neighbors in the Village

PLAY and SING the notes below in the key of D Major, following the instructions on "Cobblestone Streets" on page 21.

Play each line twice, or as many times as you need for it to be easy and fluent, using 1) your right hand; 2) left hand; and 3) copy-hands.

Where is *do* on this page of music? _____

4.

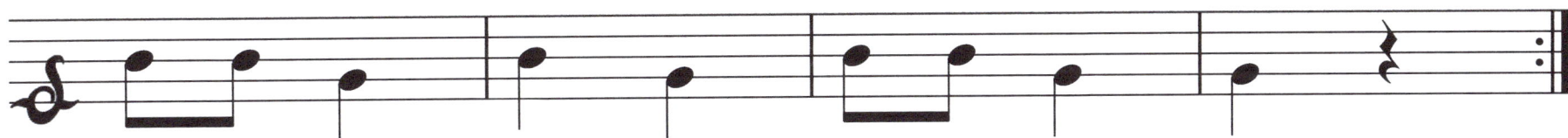

5.

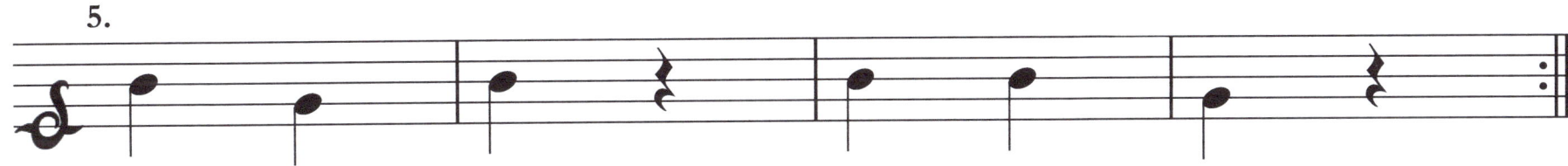

6.

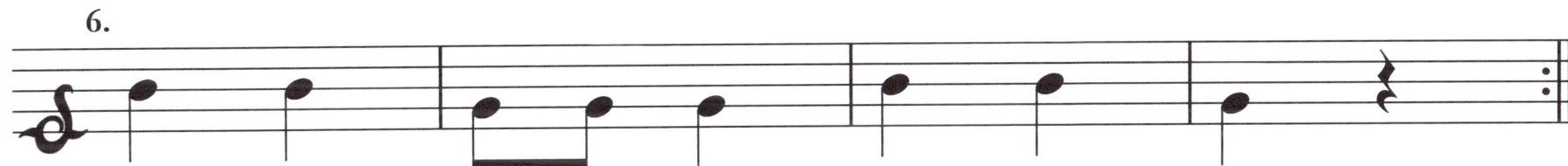

7.

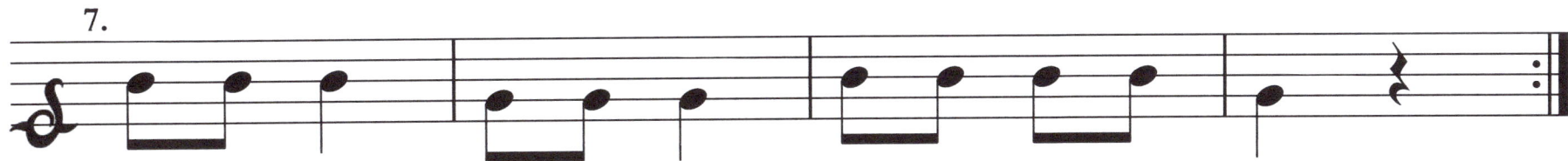

RHYTHM PUZZLE: All Around the Buttercup

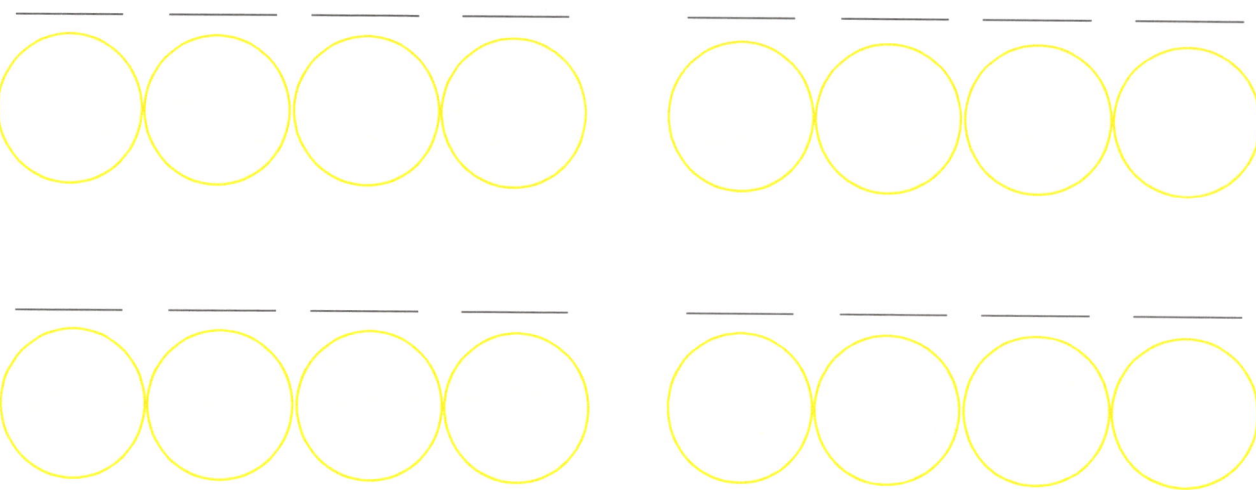

RHYTHM PUZZLE: Naughty Kitty Cat

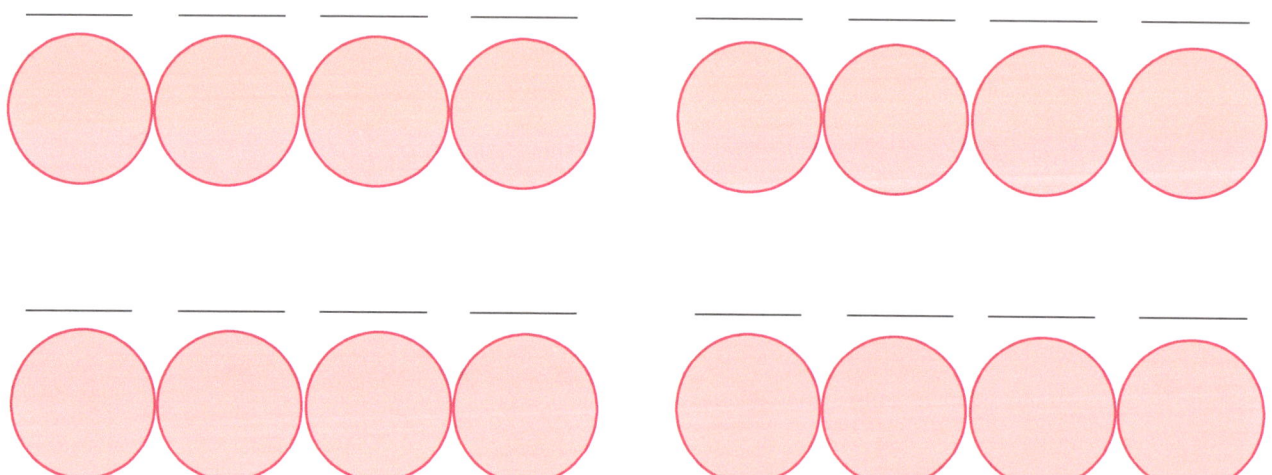

Echo in the Pines

Play and sing the notes below in the key of D Major. Use "copy-hands" as before, preparing the right and left hand individually as needed.

Play each line twice, or as many times as you need for it to be easy and fluent.

Do is in a surprising location on this page. How would you describe where it is? _____

Make sure to SING while you are playing!

8.

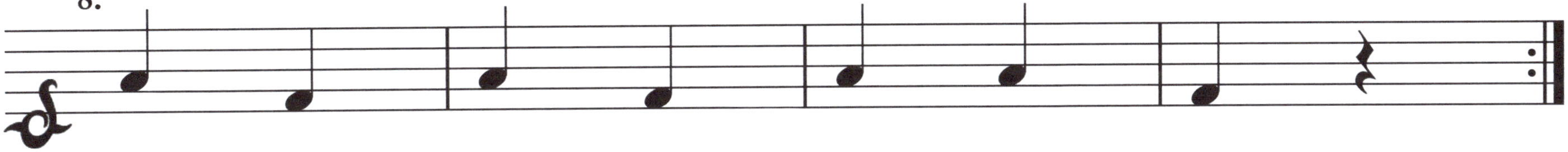

9.

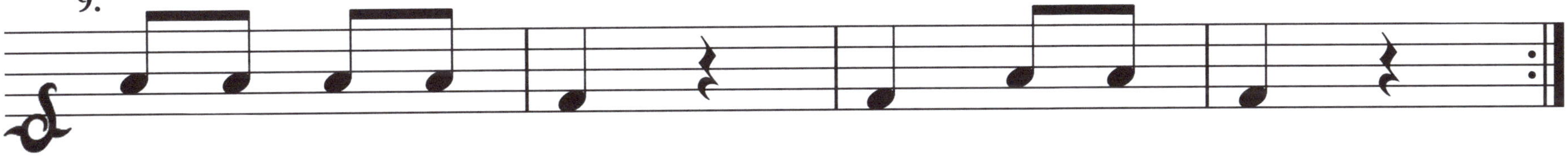

10.

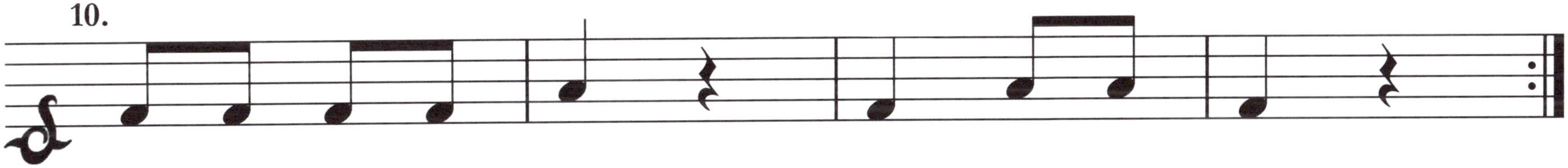

11.

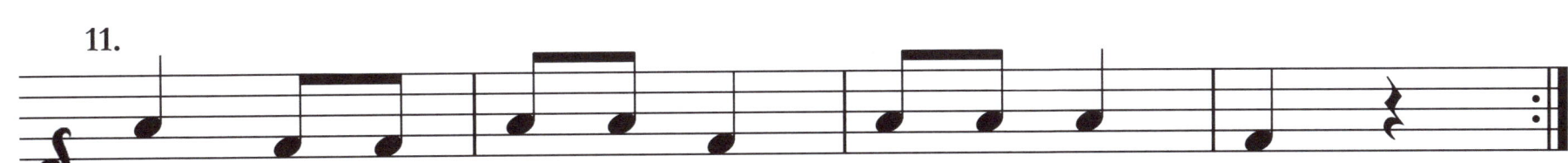

25

PIANO GAME: HOPPING FROG

Objective: Easily and quickly locating each white key.

FROGS IN THE CENOTE

1. Stand in front of the piano, moving the bench out of the way. Practice finding the note "F" on the piano, using the third finger of the RIGHT hand. Use the wrist to lift the hand. This is the frog!

2. Now do the same thing with the LEFT hand.

3. LEAPFROG: Use both hands, alternating left-right-left-right.

THE WAITING SNAKE

1. To play the game, start at the LOWEST F, then hop from F to F up to the very TOP of the piano. When you reach the top, turn around and go back down again, still hopping on "F" ...

2. But now, your partner will simultaneously begin a rapid descending white-key scale starting from the highest note. This is the snake. Don't let it "catch" you!

Try hopping back down the keyboard using your left hand, right hand, and "leapfrog" style. What is the fastest way for you to escape the snake?

Once F is mastered, play the same game with the remaining notes, in the following order:

D	Deer	B	Bobcat
C	Cricket	G	Grasshopper
E	Emu	A	Antelope

For the partner: The notes and fingering of your downward descent don't matter, as long as it gives the basic idea of slithering down the keys. But do actually finger the notes indivdually, rather than using a glissando.

A cenote ("say-note-ay") is a natural, deep pit formed by the collapse of limestone bedrock, exposing the water from underground rivers and cave systems below. Cenotes are common in Mexico's Yucatán Peninsula, and were sacred to the ancient Maya as water sources and portals to the underworld.

Afternoon Seagulls

This and subsequent exercises are played in the key of D Major, singing the solfege while playing.

Each line should be played twice, or as many times as needed for it to be easy and fluent.

On what number space is do? _____

12.

13.

14.

15.

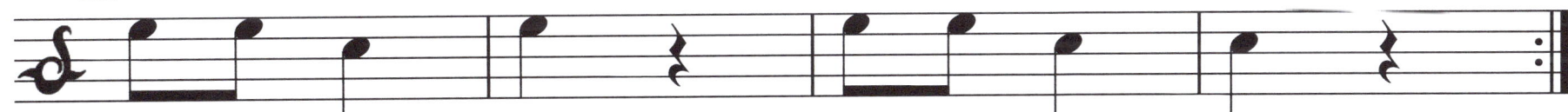

BRIDGES & TUNNELS:
FINGERING THE D SCALE

THE RIGHT HAND

In order to a full scale smoothly and fluently, we will the SHORTEST finger (i.e. the thumb) will tunnel underneath the TALLEST finger (third finger), which acts as a bridge. Let's do the ascending scale first.

Enter your age here: _____ . This is how many times a day you will play the scale.

1 2 3 1 2 3 4 5

When you are ready, learn the descending scale! Simply do the same pattern in reverse, following the arrow below the fingerings.

THE LEFT HAND

Again when you are ready, learn the same scale using the LEFT hand, going both up and down.

5 4 3 2 1 3 2 1

CHALLENGE (bonus): Can you put both hands together?

28

Morning Bells

Concept: Adding DO, with uniform note values

 Remember to SING while you are playing!

16.

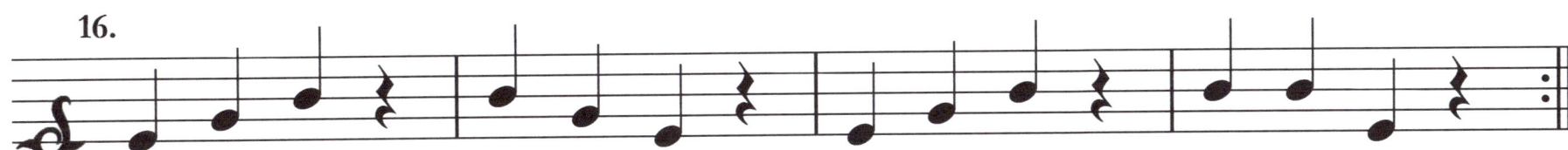

17.

18.

19.

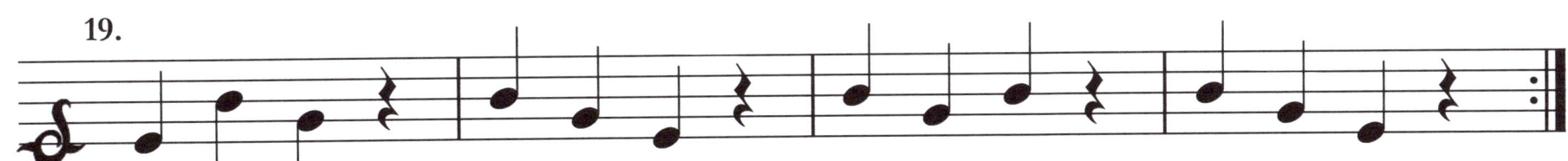

DOWN THE RABBIT HOLE, PART I

Text adapted from Alice in Wonderland, by Lewis Carroll

Objective: Navigating the keyboard; coordinating a musical line across both hands

On a summer day, Alice grew sleepy as she and her sister were reading on a river bank, when suddenly a White Rabbit hurried by her, taking a watch from the pocket of his fancy coat and uttering, "Oh, dear! Oh dear! I shall be late!"

Burning with curiosity — for she had never seen a rabbit with a coat, nor a watch before — Alice jumped up and followed him across the field of daisies, just as he popped down into a large rabbit hole.

And down went Alice after him! As you may have guessed, this was a magical rabbit hole, leading not to the other side of the earth as Alice imagined, but to an underground Wonderland where many adventures awaited her.

As Alice floated DOWN, DOWN, DOWN, she noticed there were bookshelves and cupboards, as well as maps and pictures hanging on the walls of the rabbit hole. She even picked up a jar of orange marmalade off a shelf, but alas—it was empty!

So Curious!

A DREAMY AFTERNOON

Play the natural half-steps on the piano up and down slowly in a loop, many times (at least four). Use the sustain pedal.

THE RABBIT APPEARS

Play those two pairs of notes staccato, as two clusters.

DOWN THE RABBIT HOLE!

Using these same, notes, play a cascade all the way down the piano, from highest to lowest. Cross your hands over each other, starting with the right hand, to create a smooth line without pauses. Practice this until it is fluent and seamless.

There are lots of ways to go down a magical rabbit hole. Explore these musical ideas!

Dynamics: Get gradually softer | Stay the same | Get gradually louder

Tempo: Get gradually slower | Stay the same | Get gradually faster

The Landing: Does Alice land softly on a furry rug, or with a kerplunk?

Continue exploring this musical story. Create your own ideas!

A Dreamy Afternoon

The Rabbit Appears

Down the Rabbit Hole!

30

Overlooking the Lake

Concept: Tonic on the 2nd line; reading DMS with rhythms

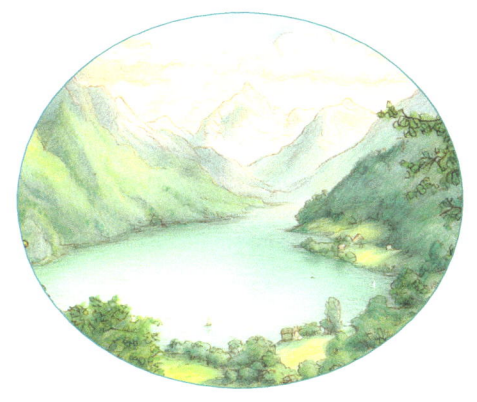

Learning Tip

Each day, play through the note-reading page you've most recently graduated, to refresh your skills. Then work on your new assignment.

On what number line is *do*? _______

20.

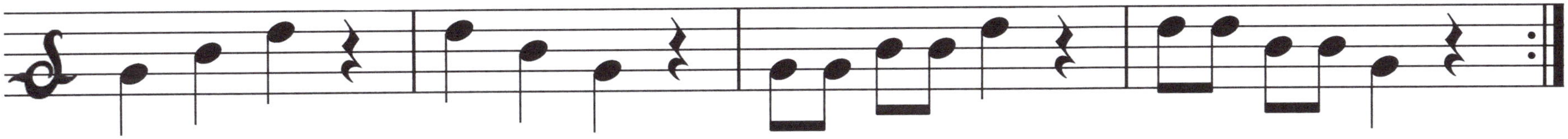

21.

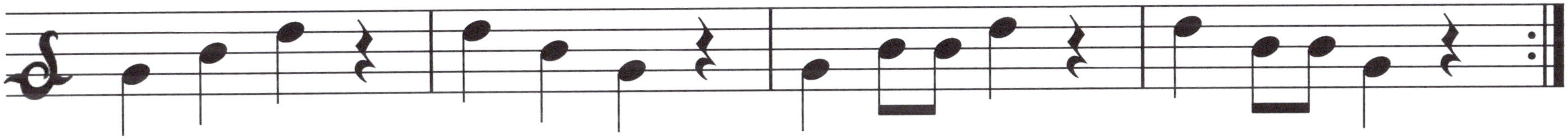

22.

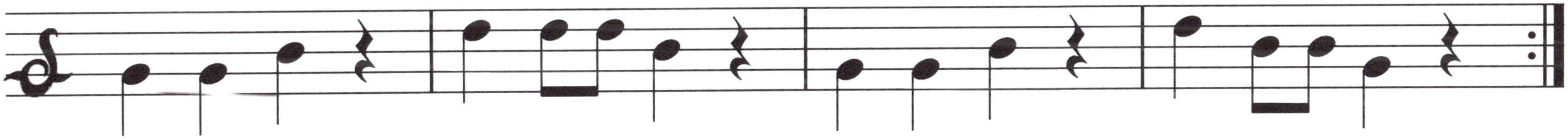

23.

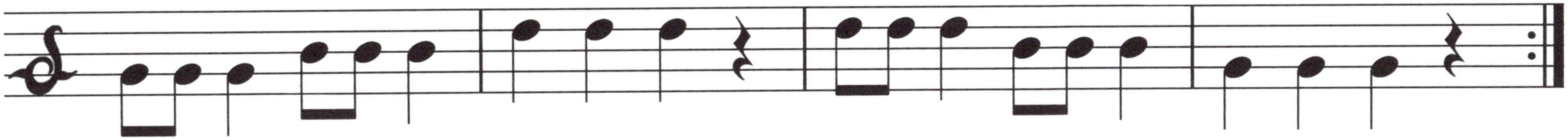

DOWN THE RABBIT HOLE, PART II

Objective: Coordinating a musical line across both hands

DOWN THE RABBIT HOLE, REVISITED

You'll be creating story as before – 1) The Dreamy Afternoon, 2) The Rabbit Appears, and 3) Down the Rabbit Hole! – but this time using different notes. If the previous pattern was "the white pattern," we can call this the "the checkered pattern."

What musical choices would you like to make this time? Can you find different choices from the ones you made last time?

"DRINK ME"

Alice went back to the table, and this time she found a little bottle on it ("which certainly was not here before," said Alice), and tied round the neck was a paper label, with the words, "DRINK ME" beautifully printed on it in large letters.

Alice ventured to taste it, and soon found herself only ten inches high — the right size for going through the little door into the garden.

This pattern skips exactly one key between each key you play. This is called a "whole-tone" scale.

Play all of the notes within a single octave above middle C, going up and down the scale.

THE RABBIT RUNS OFF TO THE DUCHESS

After a time, Alice heard a little pattering of feet in the distance. It was the White Rabbit returning, splendidly dressed, with a pair of white kid gloves in one hand and a large fan in the other: he came trotting along in a great hurry, muttering to himself, "Oh! The Duchess, the Duchess! Oh, won't she be savage if I've kept her waiting!" Then he scurried away into the darkness as hard as he could go.

Play the whole-tone scale quickly from the top of the piano, all the way down to the bottom, crossing each hand over the other.

Two Kittens

On what number space is *do*? _____

 Make sure to SING while you are playing!

24.

25.

26.

27.

THE HAUNTED MANSION

Mark these notes in the *highest* octave of the piano. They will serve as a visual template.

CREAKS IN THE HOUSE

Play the FIRST and FOURTH fingers of each hand together in each octave of the piano. Use the closest hand to play each pair of notes.

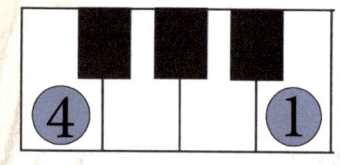  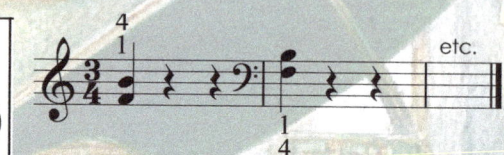

HAUNTED MELODY

1. The Haunted melody uses all the notes inside the "Creaks" interval! Play this melody in every octave.

2. Something is stirring in the basement! SUSTAIN the "Creak" sound in the LEFT hand while playing the Haunted Melody with the RIGHT hand.

   Move the melody into various octaves. The left hand can stay in one place or move, as you wish.

 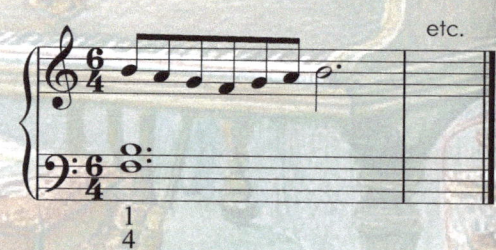

UH OH ... IT'S IN THE HOUSE!

Play the "Creaks" sound twice with BOTH hands at the same time. Move the RIGHT hand (only) up an octave each time, getting louder and louder.

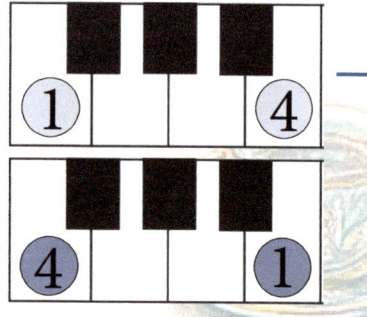 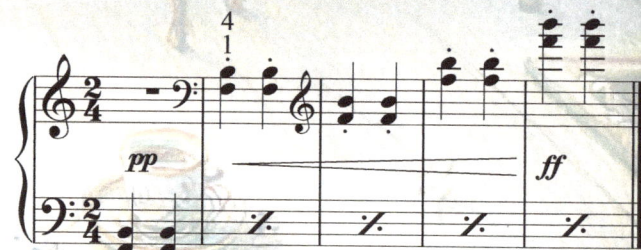

34

Late for a Very Important Date

Where is *do*? _____

28.

29.

30.

31.

BATS IN THE BELFRY

PIANO FLASHCARDS

Objective: Visually recognizing and naming each of the white keys.

Preparation: Remove the two Piano Flash Card pages (page 57) and cut out the flash cards along the dotted lines.

These flash cards can be used in the normal way, or you can make them more interesting and fun using the following game:

1. The practice partner shows the student a flash card. The student responds with the name of the note.

2. **But watch out ... there are TWO special notes. These notes are how you earn points.**

   - If the note is "A," do NOT say the note name. Instead, form your arms into a steeple shape, like the letter A. (A *belfry* is the part of a church tower, or steeple, where the bells are located.)

   - If the note is "B," do NOT say the note name. Instead, hold out your wings like bat wings.

If you make a mistake on any note name OR movement, your partner gets one point.

The game is over when you get EIGHT points or the partner gets FOUR points — whichever happens first.

More Gameplay Options

VERSION 1: Choose different notes for points. Create a unique movement for each one.

VERSION 2: PLAY the notes on the piano *as well as* saying them out loud.

VERSION 3: Play the game as a group, with students taking individual turns. Students may play individually for points, or they may play in teams, with the whole team gaining or losing points. *If playing with a mixed-level group, the more advanced students can play flashcards from a different deck, e.g. showing treble or bass clef notes notated on the staff.*

36

The Reflecting Pool

Concept: Adding RE; using steps and skips to navigate visually and to audiate the notes

1. Where is do? _____

2. Speak through the exercise using the following four choices: "step up," "step down," "skip up," and "skip down."

3. Use this awareness of steps and skips to easily play the exercise below. This is easier than memorizing the location of all the notes!

32.

33.

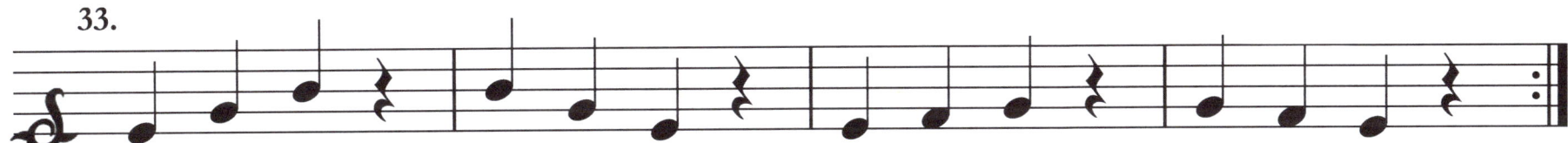

34.

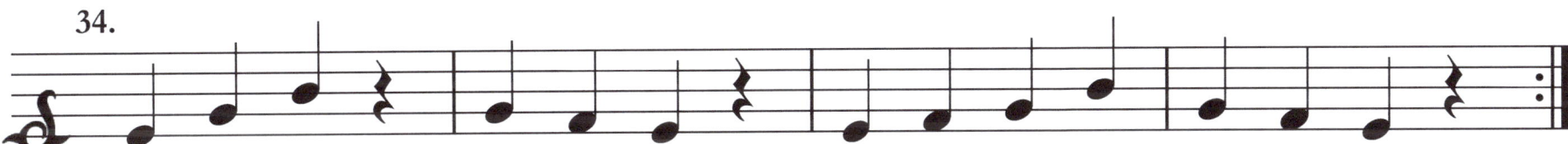

35.

36.

THE MAGIC HARP

Objective: Introducing the concept of a chord; playing arpeggios using correct pianistic fingering; coordinating a musical line across both hands

The Dagda had many wonderful magical possessions. But perhaps his greatest treasure was his harp, Uaithne. It was made of oak and richly decorated, and only the Dagda could get music from it strings. He could make anyone who heard it laugh for joy, or weep with sorrow, and the playing of this harp made the seasons come in the correct order.

– Irish legend

Vocabulary

Chord: Three or more notes which are related to each other by consecutive skips, or *thirds*. Chords can be played *blocked* (all together) or *broken* (the notes played sequentially in an infinite variety of ways). They may even be moved into different octaves!

Triad: A chord of three notes, consisting of a given note (the *root*) with a *third* and *fifth* above it.

Arpeggio: The notes of a chord, played *sequentially* (rather than simultaneously) and *in order* (although some notes may be skipped). The word "arpeggio" comes from the word "harp" in Italian!

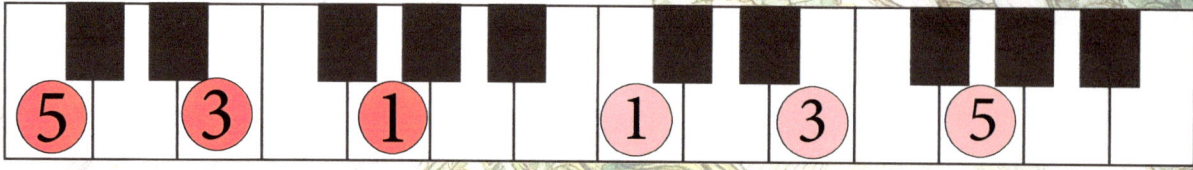

1. Place the lowest finger of both hands on C. Make sure that one finger is on each key.

2. Play an arpeggio across both hands, starting with the left hand, using the fingering above.

3. Now lift your hands from the wrists, and move them a tiny bit to the right, so that both bottom fingers are on D. Play the same pattern on the new set of notes.

4. Continue up the scale, using only the white keys. You will finish with both hands one octave higher, on the note C.

Practice this sequence until it is fluent and easy. Do a little bit each day.

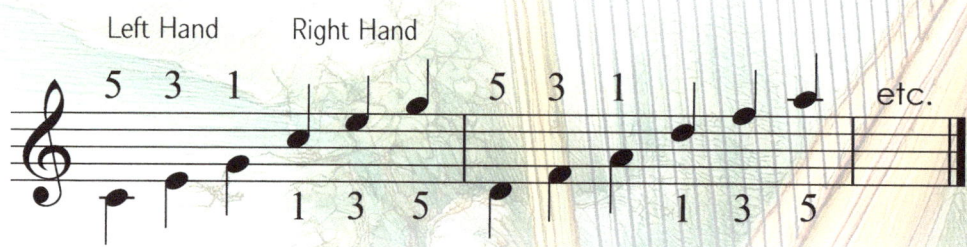

When you are ready, try a double arpeggio — four octaves within each pattern, alternating hands. Move this pattern up the scale until both hands are back on C.

38

First Steps Into the Meadow

1. Where is do? _____

2. Speak through the exercise using the following four choices: "step up," "step down," "skip up," and "skip down."

3. Use this awareness of steps and skips to play the exercise.

37.

38.

39.

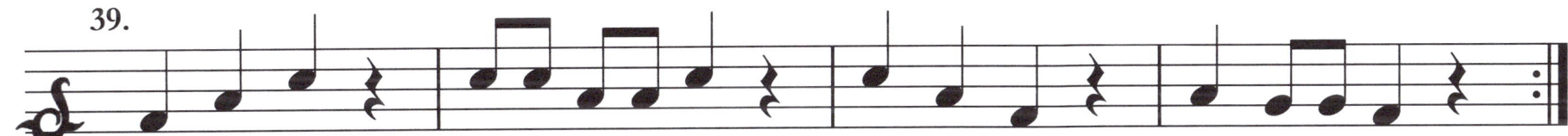

40.

HALF STEPS & WHOLE STEPS

We say that two adjacent keys on the piano are a *half step* (*semitone*) apart. These adjacent notes may be a white and black key, or two white keys. You might recognize the sound of a half-step as the sound of approaching danger from the movie "Jaws."

When two keys on the piano are separated by another key, this is called a *whole step* (*tone*). Notice the different sound of this interval — a bit more like ... butterflies?

GUESS THE WORD

1. Both the partner and the student choose a mystery word and write a blank for each letter.

2. The partner plays a half- or whole-step within view of the student. The student identifies the interval. If they are right, they may guess one letter. If they are wrong, the parent may guess one letter.

Win the game by being the first to correctly guess the other person's word!

TIC TAC TOE

Draw a tic-tac-toe grid, or use the board at the right with ten tiles of two colors.

1. The parent plays a half or whole step on the piano, within view of the student.

2. For each correctly identified half- or whole-step, the student may place their tile in any of the squares. For each misidentified half- or whole-step, the parent may place their own tile.

The winner is whoever gets three in a row — horizontally, vertically, or diagonally.

GAMEPLAY OPTIONS FOR BOTH GAMES:

Version 1: The student can see the notes being played.

Version 2: The parent chooses a *starting* note and an *interval* (half step or whole step). The student must play the correct *second* note.

Version 3: The student identifies the half or whole step by ear.

Three examples of half steps

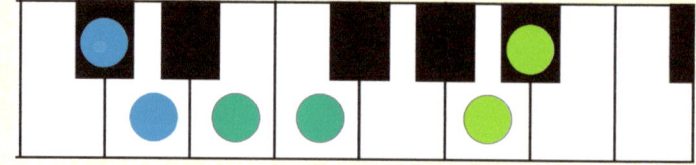

Three examples of whole steps

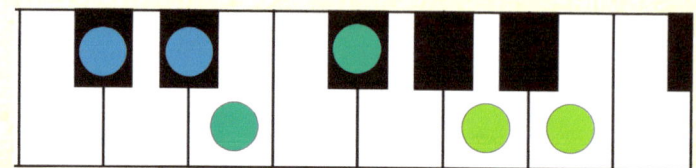

Barnyard Hoedown

41.

42.

43.

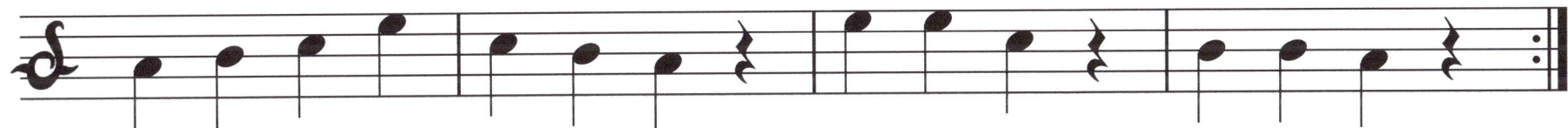

44.

45.

THE BASILISK

Objective: Applying the concept of half-and whole steps; coordinating the hands in a novel way

In ancient Greek and Roman myths, the basilisk is a magical, deadly serpent. Anyone who looks directly into its eyes is instantly killed or turned to stone. Even the bravest warriors may fall victim to its gaze without ever drawing a weapon. The weasel destroys the basilisk with its odor; in some legends it may also be defeated by showing it its own reflection.

CHOOSE THE MELODY

1. Play THREE notes in a pattern of half and whole steps. Try a few different patterns until you find the most interesting sound. Mark these notes with erasers to use as a template in the next step.

2. Play this sequence of notes in various octaves on the piano.

3. Now remove the erasers (if you used them) and practice finding the pattern again.

Example pattern of half and whole steps

ADD THE SUSPENSE

Now experiment with a note to play in the left hand, which will sustain underneath your pattern.

For the CREEPIEST POSSIBLE SOUND, choose a note that is different from the three notes played in your right hand.

Now play the two-hand pattern in different places on the piano, moving both notes.

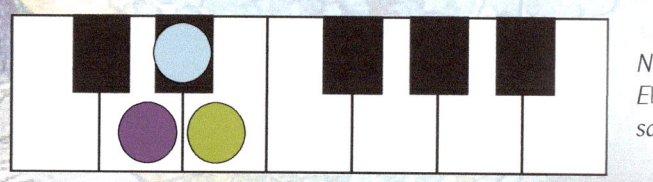

Note: The note $E\flat$ (E flat) is the same as $D\sharp$.

Adding the suspense

CREATE THE FORESHADOWING

Foreshadowing is when you sense danger approaching.

Repeat each melody note twice for each time you play the bass note. Then move the pattern up one octave at a time, keeping the bass note the same.

What other ideas would you like to add?

The foreshadowing

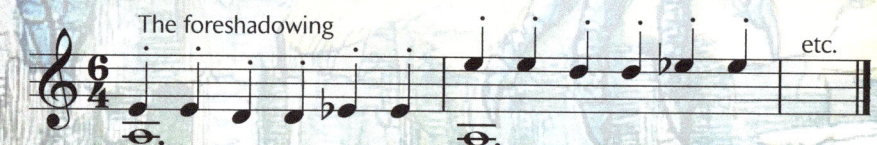

Further Merriment at the Hoedown

46.

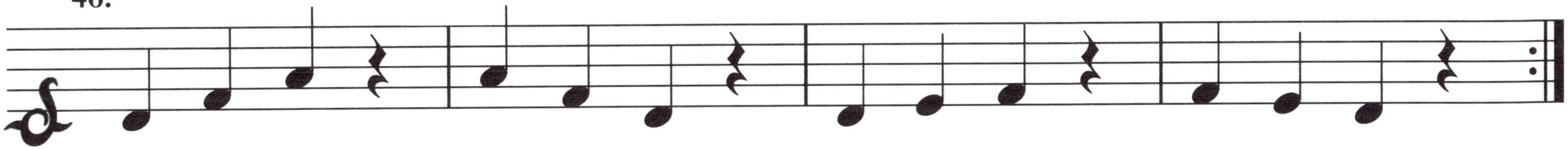

47.

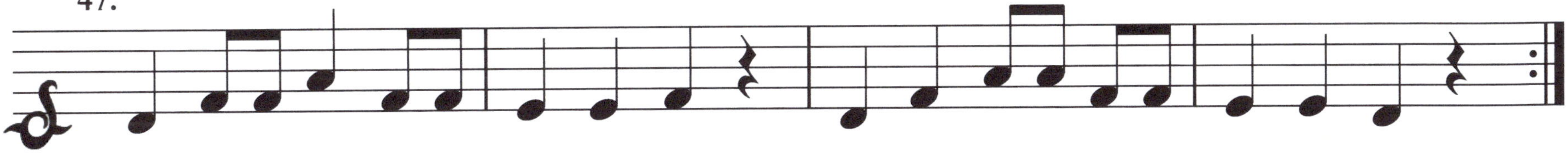

48.

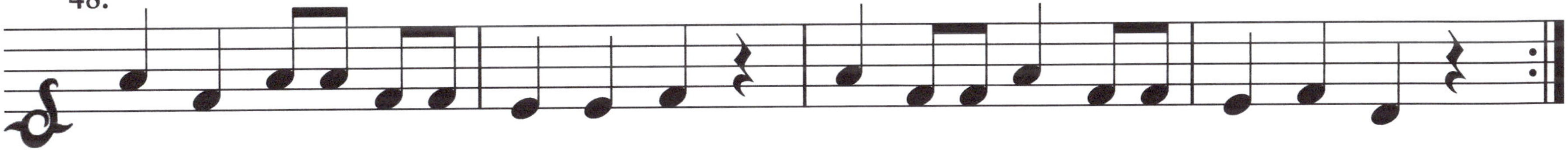

49.

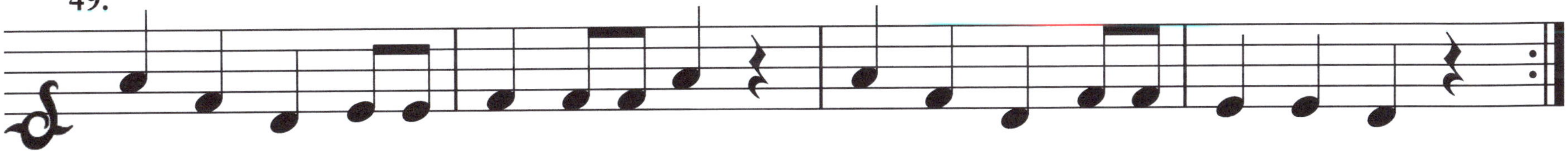

43

CATS IN THE CATHEDRAL, PART I

Objective: To notice the interaction of various notes with a tonic pedal tone.

PRELUDE IN C

1. The partner plays a steady beat on low C, holding down the sustain pedal.

2. The student plays Cs moving upward on the piano, aligned with the beat.

THE CATS EXPLORE

Find the note C on the piano.

The partner plays a steady beat on this note, holding down the sustain pedal. Meanwile, the student improvises on white keys of their choice, using just the third (middle) finger of the hand to play the various notes. As some notes are elongated, musical phrases will arise naturally.

Work toward keeping the melody aligned with the beat. Playing 2-beat melody notes in the beginning is helpful.

CAT HAIKU

Choose a set of notes to accompany the poem "Cats in the Cathedral, Part II" on page 46. Once you've chosen them, write the note names on the lines provided next to the poem. Two notes are filled in for you.

The last note of each phrase is longer, and can be played for any number of beats. The bass will continue its steady beat during this time.

Cats in the Cathedral (example — notes chosen by student)

Cat Haiku (example — notes chosen by student)

Bonus activity: Listen to "Für Alina," by Estonian composer Arvo Pärt, performed by Tähe-Lee Liiv.

"Every note is a blade of grass. And every blade of grass is a flower." – Arvo Pärt

44

Concepts: Moving between RE and SO; novel rest placements

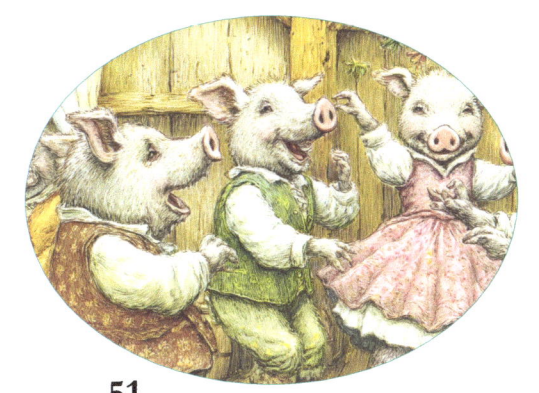

The Hogs Go Wild

51.

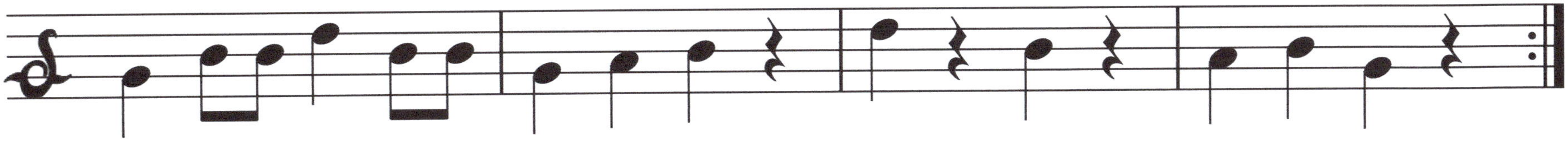

52.

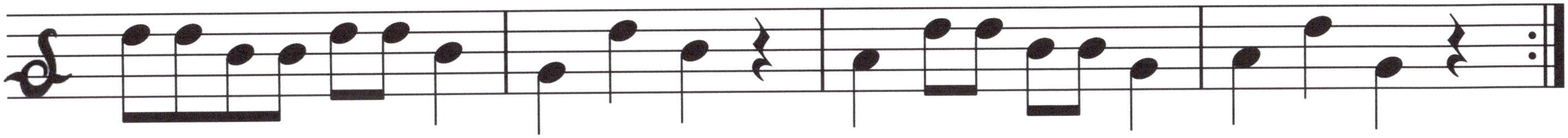

53.

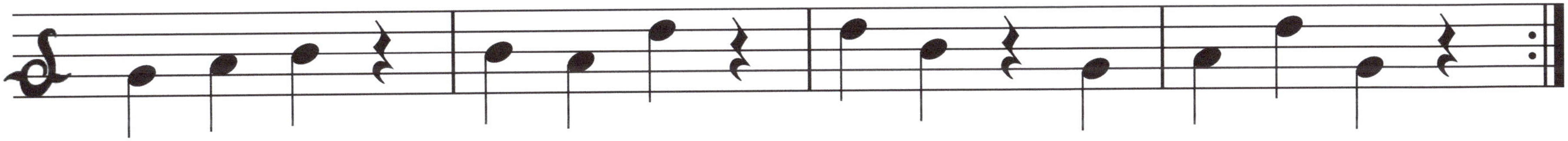

54.

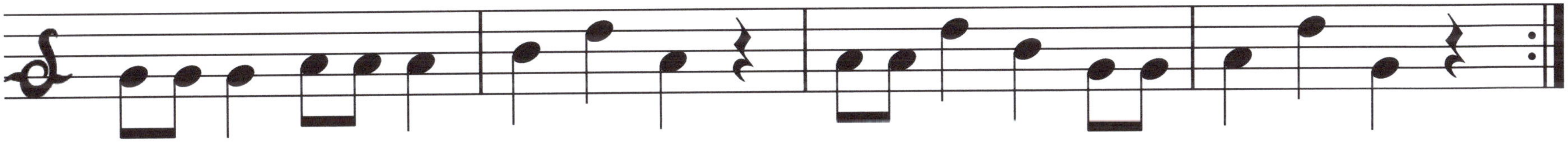

55.

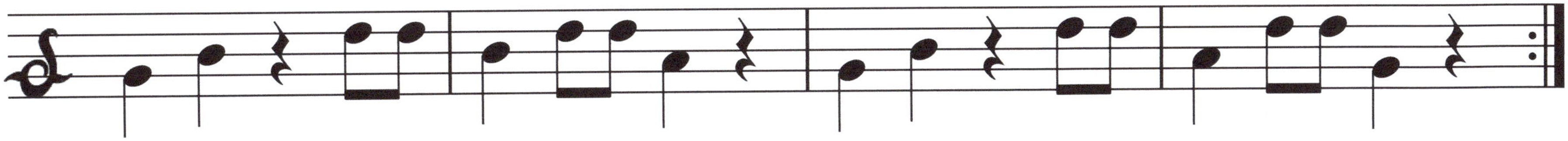

CATS IN THE CATHEDRAL, PART II

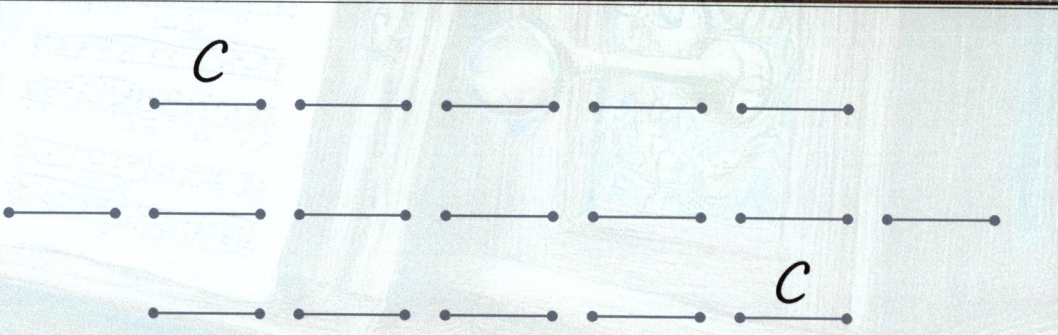

Cathedral at night

Cats appear from all around

A chorus of cats.

TUXEDO CAT AWAKENS

Instead of just one note in the accompaniment, play a fifth (C and G). The student improvises on white key notes as before.

The partner can play the bass notes using their right hand with outside fingers (1 and 5). Eventually the student may play their own bass, using the left hand with the same fingers in reverse.

Tuxedo Cat Awakens

MELODIOUS SCALE

A *third* is played using the thumb and third finger of the right hand. The wrist should lift the hand each time, with the fingers draping as the wrist lifts, then falling gently on the keys.

1. Play thirds going up the C scale, then back down again.

2. Now do the same thing while the partner repeats the C in the bass.

Melodious Scale

CHORUS OF CATS

Now add thirds to the haiku that you just created.

A Chorus of Cats

46

An Unexpected Friendship

56.

57.

58.

59.

60.

Celebration in the Forest

61.

62.

63.

64.

65.

Musical Toolkit

The Musical Staff

The Kaleidoscopes Rhythm System

Duple Meter		
Quarter note	♩	TA
8th notes	♫	TA TE
16th notes	♬♬	ta ka te ka
32nd notes		ta ma ka ma te ma ka ma

Triple Meter		
Quarter note	♩	TA
8th notes		TA TU TI
16th notes		ta ka tu ka ti ka
32nd notes		ta ma ka ma tu ma ka ma ti ma ka ma

51

Kaleidoscopes Rhythm System (back)

Rhythm Flashcards page 1 (back)

Rhythm Flashcards page 2 (back)

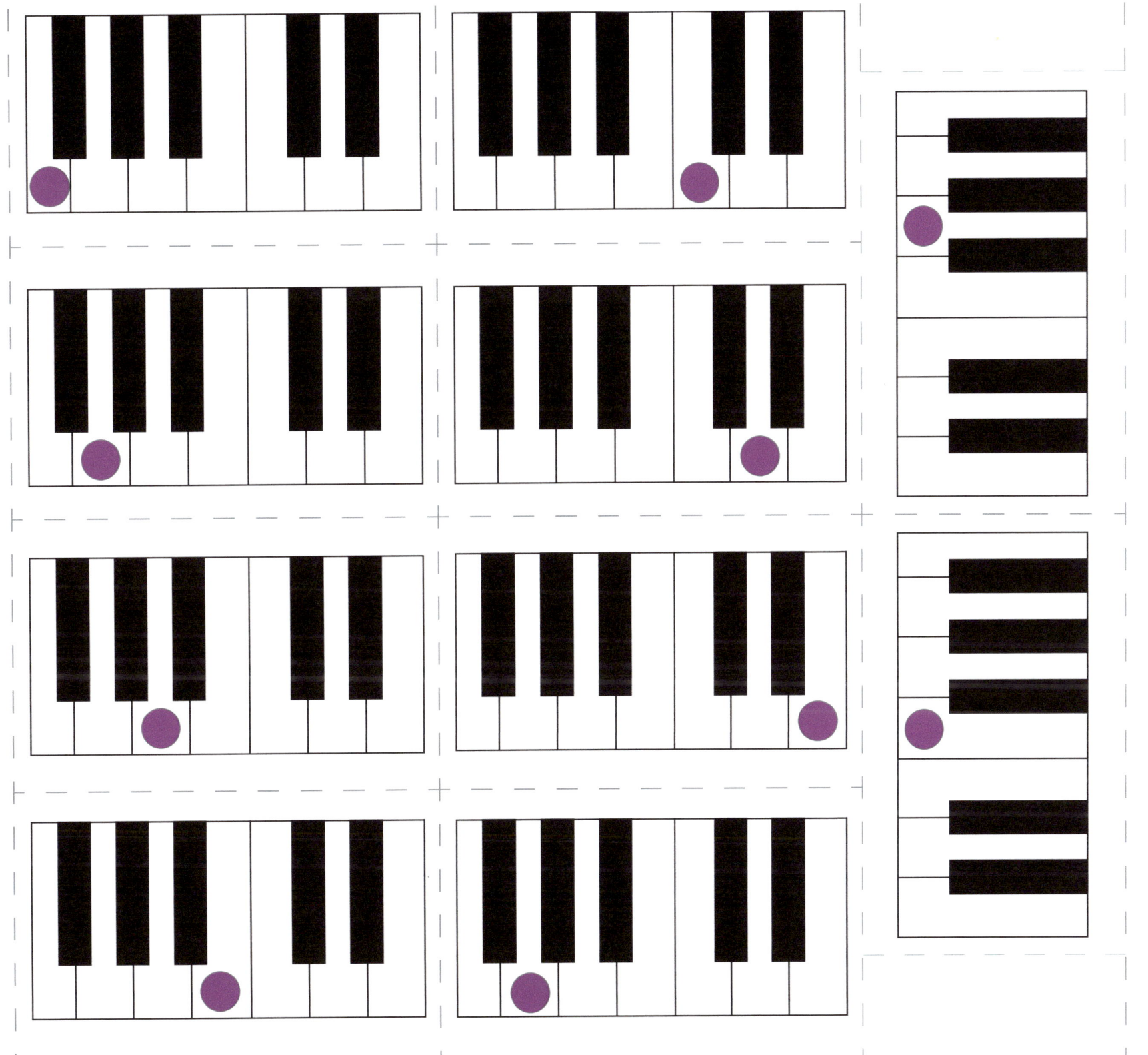

A C F

D G

B E A

G B

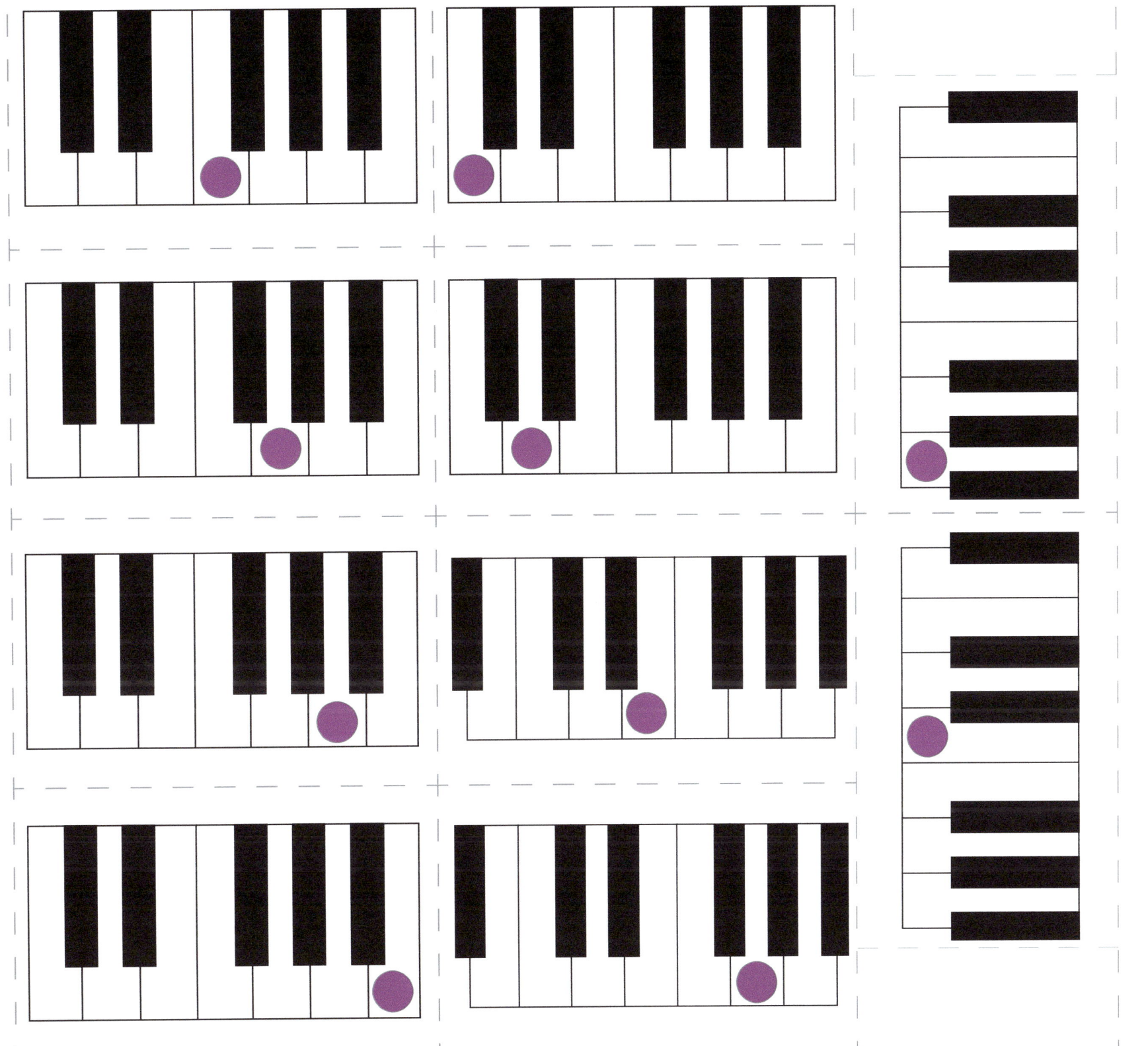

A C F

D G

E E A

G B

HOLLIE THOMAS
EDUCATOR, PIANIST & COMPOSER

Hollie Thomas is an award-winning composer, pianist, and educator dedicated to helping musicians deepen their musical understanding and chord prowess through creative play on the piano. Hollie's compositions have received several awards, most notably the International League of Women Composers Ellen Taaffe Zwilich Award for her setting of Robert Frost's "Fire and Ice."

As a pianist, Hollie has performed worldwide in classical and modern chamber groups; for cabaret, theater, and dance; and as with eclectic pop/rock artists and bands including David Garza, the Kevin McCormick Ensemble, Mistress Stephanie & Her Melodic Cat, Deep Edward, The Jellydots, and Future Clouds & Radar.

Hollie holds a Bachelor or Arts in Music Composition, studying composition with Dr. Michael Woods and Dr. Jerry Hatley; and studied classical piano performance with Dr. Betty Kirk, and Dr. Timothy Woolsey, and Hugh E. Thompson, Sr.

Following a life-changing trip to Kiev, Ukraine in 1990, Hollie obtained her Masters of Education in the field of Linguistic Acquisition, and spent 10 years as an intensive English as a Second Language instructor and a curriculum developer for the English Language Center at the University of Texas at Austin.

In 2003, Hollie made the decision to focus full-time on her private music teaching studio. Little did she imagine that her experience teaching language would exert a decisive influence, providing the vision for a piano teaching methodology which would more closely mirror language acquisition, crafted over the next two decades. Her teaching process transforms traditional technique teaching into a creative process that is fundamentally sourced from an understanding of harmony and composition.

Elise Winters
Educator, Violinist & Pedagogue

Elise is the author of *Kaleidoscopes* series for violin, viola and cello, which was developed over two decades and blends Montessori and Kodaly principles within a Suzuki framework. Her teacher trainings in this ground-breaking method have received rave reviews from teachers in the United States, Canada, England, and Australia.

A graduate *summa cum laude* from Rice University and holding a Master of Social Work from the University of Texas, Elise's interests and training extend to developmental psychology, linguistics, cognition, communication, biomechanics, and contemplative dance. This diverse background has placed her in a unique position to write an inter-disciplinary, child-focused instrumental method.

As a violinist, Elise has performed as a member of the Austin Symphony, Austin Lyric Opera, and the Grammy Award-winning Conspirare choir. She has been featured as a soloist with Austin Chamber Music Center, the Victoria Bach Festival, and as guest concertmistress of La Follia Austin Baroque. An avid chamber musician, she performed for five years with the Austin String Quartet alongside the principals of the Austin Symphony, and served as Education Director of Chamber Music in Public Schools (CHAMPS) program in Austin, Texas.

She studied violin with renowned teacher trainer Ronda Cole and with Elisabeth Adkins, Assistant Concertmaster of the National Symphony.

Elise completed her 3-year Kodaly training at Indiana University Jacobs School of Music under Brent Gault, Georgia Newlin, and Diana Pannell; and received training in Music Together under Devi Borton.

Her Suzuki teacher trainers include Ronda Cole, Judy Bossuat-Gallic, Cathy Lee, Marilyn O'Boyle, Doris Preucil, Edward Kreitman, and Charles Krigbaum.

She is the composer of the original, whimsical piano accompaniments for the first two volumes of the book, and is the director of the Music Theory program at Enchanted Wood Suzuki Studio in Austin, Texas.